MACMILLAN MASTER GUIDES
OTHELLO
BY WILLIAM SHAKESPEARE

TONY BROMHAM

with an Introduction by
HAROLD BROOKS

MACMILLAN

First published 1988 by
MACMILLAN PRESS LTD
Houndmills, Basingstoke, Hampshire RG21 6XS
and London
Companies and representatives
throughout the world

ISBN 0–333–40407–6

A catalogue record for this book is available
from the British Library.

13 12 11 10 9 8 7 6 5
05 04 03 02 01 00 99 98

Printed in Malaysia

CONTENTS

GENERAL EDITOR'S PREFACE

The aim of the Macmillan Master Guides is to help you to appreciate the book you are studying by providing information about it and by suggesting ways of reading and thinking about it which will lead to a fuller understanding. The section on the writer's life and background has been designed to illustrate those aspects of the writer's life which have influenced the work, and to place it in its personal and literary context. The summaries and critical commentary are of special importance in that each brief summary of the action is followed by an examination of the significant critical points. The space which might have been given to repetitive explanatory notes has been devoted to a detailed analysis of the kind of passage which might confront you in an examination. Literary criticism is concerned with both the broader aspects of the work being studied and with its detail. The ideas which meet us in reading a great work of literature, and their relevance to us today, are an essential part of our study, and our Guides look at the thought of their subject in some detail. But just as essential is the craft with which the writer has constructed his work of art, and this may be considered under several technical headings – characterisation, language, style and stagecraft, for example.

The authors of these Guides are all teachers and writers of wide experience, and they have chosen to write about books they admire and know well in the belief that they can communicate their admiration to you. But you yourself must read and know intimately the book you are studying. No one can do that for you. You should see this book as a lamp-post. Use it to shed light, not to lean against. If you know your text and know what it is saying about life, and how it says it, then you will enjoy it, and there is no better way of passing an examination in literature.

JAMES GIBSON

AN INTRODUCTION TO THE STUDY OF SHAKESPEARE'S PLAYS

A play as a work of art exists to the full only when performed. It must hold the audience's attention throughout the performance, and, unlike a novel, it can't be put down and taken up again. It is important to experience the play as if you are seeing it on the stage for the first time, and you should begin by reading it straight through. Shakespeare builds a play in dramatic units which may be divided into smaller subdivisions, or episodes, marked off by exits and entrances and lasting as long as the same actors are on the stage. Study it unit by unit.

The first unit provides the exposition which is designed to put the audience into the picture. In the second unit we see the forward movement of the play as one situation changes into another. The last unit in a tragedy or a tragical play will bring the catastrophe, and in comedy — and some of the history plays — an unravelling of the complications, what is called a *dénouement*.

The onward movement of the play from start to finish is its progressive structure. We see the chain of cause and effect (the plot) and the progressive revelation and development of character. The people, their characters and their motives drive the plot forward in a series of scenes which are carefully planned to give variety of pace and excitement. We notice fast-moving and slower-moving episodes, tension mounting and slackening, and alternative fear and hope for the characters we favour. Full-stage scenes, such as stately councils and processions or turbulent mobs, contrast with scenes of small groups or even single speakers. Each of the scenes presents a deed or event which changes the situation. In performances, entrances and exits and stage actions are physical facts, with more impact than on the page. That impact Shakespeare relied upon, and we must restore it by an effort of the imagination.

Shakespeare's language is just as diverse. Quickfire dialogue is followed by long speeches, and verse changes to prose. There is a wide range of speech — formal, colloquial, dialect, 'Mummerset' and the broken English of foreigners, for example. Songs, instrumental music, and the noise of battle, revelry and tempest, all extend the range of dramatic expression. The dramatic use of language is enhanced by skilful stagecraft, by costumes, by properties such as beds, swords and Yorick's skull, by such stage business as kneeling, embracing and giving money, and by use of such features of the stage structure as the balcony and the trapdoor.

By these means Shakespeare's people are brought vividly to life and cleverly individualised. But though they have much to tell us about human nature, we must never forget that they are characters in a play, not in real life. And remember, they exist to enact the play, not the play to portray *them*.

Shakespeare groups his characters so that they form a pattern, and it is useful to draw a diagram showing this. Sometimes a linking character has dealings with each group. The pattern of persons belongs to the symmetric structure of the play, and its dramatic unity is reinforced and enriched by a pattern of resemblances and contrasts; for instance, between characters, scenes, recurrent kinds of imagery, and words. It is not enough just to notice a feature that belongs to the symmetric structure, you should ask what its relevance is to the play as a whole and to the play's ideas.

These ideas and the dramatising of them in a central theme, or several related to each other, are a principal source of the dramatic unity. In order to see what themes are present and important, look, as before, for pattern. Observe the place in it of the leading character. In tragedy this will be the protagonist, in comedy heroes and heroines, together with those in conflict or contrast with them. In *Henry IV Part I*, Prince Hal is being educated for kingship and has a correct estimate of honour, while Falstaff despises honour, and Hotspur makes an idol of it. Pick out the episodes of great intensity as, for example, in *King Lear* where the theme of spiritual blindness is objectified in the blinding of Gloucester, and similarly, note the emphases given by dramatic poetry as in Prospero's 'Our revels now are ended . . .' or unforgettable utterances such as Lear's 'Is there any cause in Nature that makes these hard hearts?' Striking stage-pictures such as that of Hamlet behind the King at prayer will point to leading themes, as will all the parallels and recurrences, including those of phrase and imagery. See whether, in the play you are studying, themes known to be favourites with Shakespeare are prominent, themes such as those of order and disorder, relationships disrupted by mistakes about identity, and appearance and reality. The latter were bound to fascinate Shakespeare, whose theatrical art worked by means of illusions which pointed beyond the surface of actual life to underlying truths. In looking at themes beware of attempts to make the play fit some orthodoxy a critic believes in − Freudian perhaps, or Marxist, or dogmatic Christian theology − and remember that its ideas, though they often have a bearing on ours, are Elizabethan.

Some of Shakespeare's greatness lies in the good parts he wrote for the actors. In his demands upon them, and the opportunities he provided, he bore their professional skills in mind and made use of their physical prowess, relished by a public accustomed to judge fencing and wrestling as expertly as we today judge football and tennis. As a member of the professional group of players called the Chamberlain's Men he knew each actor he was writing for. To play his women he had highly trained boys. As paired heroines they were often contrasted, short with tall, for example, or one vivacious and enterprising, the other more conventionally feminine.

Richard Burbage, the company's leading man, was famous as a great tragic actor, and he took leading roles in seven of Shakespeare's *tragedies*. Though each of the seven has its own distinctiveness, we shall find at the centre of all of them a tragic protagonist possessing tragic greatness, not just one 'tragic flaw' but a tragic vulnerability. He will have a character which makes him unfit to cope with the tragic situations confronting him, so that his tragic errors bring down upon him tragic suffering and finally a tragic catastrophe. Normally, both the suffering and the catastrophe are far worse than he can be said to deserve, and others are engulfed in them who deserve such a fate less or not at all. Tragic terror is aroused in us because, though exceptional, he is sufficiently near to normal humankind for his fate to remind us of what can happen to human beings like ourselves, and because we see in it a combination of inexorable law and painful mystery. We recognise the principle of cause and effect where in a tragic world errors return upon those who make them, but we are also aware of the tragic disproportion between cause and effect. In a tragic world you may kick a stone and start an avalanche which will destroy you and others with you. Tragic pity is aroused in us by this disproportionate suffering, and also by all the kinds of suffering undergone by every character who has won our imaginative sympathy. Imaginative sympathy is wider than moral approval, and is felt even if suffering does seem a just and logical outcome. In addition to pity and terror we have a sense of tragic waste because catastrophe has affected so much that was great and fine. Yet we feel also a tragic exaltation. To our grief the men and women who represented those values have been destroyed, but the values themselves have been shown not to depend upon success, nor upon immunity from the worst of tragic sufferings and disaster.

Comedies have been of two main kinds, or cross-bred from the two. In critical comedies the governing aim is to bring out the absurdity or irrationality of follies and abuses, and make us laugh at them. Shakespeare's comedies often do this, but most of them belong primarily to the other kind – romantic comedy. Part of the romantic appeal is to our liking for suspense; they are dramas of averted threat, beginning in trouble and ending in joy. They appeal to the romantic senses of adventure and of wonder, and to complain that they are improbable is silly because the improbability, the marvellousness, is part of the pleasure. They dramatise stories of romantic love, accompanied by love doctrine – ideas and ideals of love. But they are plays in two tones, they are comic as well as romantic. There is often something to laugh at even in the love stories of the nobility and gentry, and just as there is high comedy in such incidents as the cross-purposes of the young Athenians in the wood, and Rosalind as 'Ganymede' teasing Orlando, there is always broad comedy for characters of lower rank. Even where one of the sub-plots has no effect on the main plot, it may take up a topic from it and present it in a more comic way.

What is there in the play to make us laugh or smile? We can distinguish many kinds of comedy it may employ. *Language* can amuse by its wit, or by absurdity, as in Bottom's malapropisms. Feste's nonsense-phrases, so fatuously admired by Sir Andrew, are deliberate, while his catechising of Olivia is clown-routine. Ass-headed Bottom embraced by the Fairy Queen is a *comic spectacle* combining costume and stage-business. His wanting to play every part is *comedy of character*. Phebe disdaining Silvius and in love with 'Ganymede', or Malvolio treating Olivia as though she had written him a love-letter is *comedy of situation*; the situation is laughably different from what Phebe or Malvolio supposes. A comic let-down or anticlimax can be devastating, as we see when Aragon, sure that he deserves Portia, chooses the silver casket only to find the portrait not of her but of a 'blinking idiot'. By *slapstick, caricature* or sheer *ridiculousness of situation*, comedy can be exaggerated into farce, which Shakespeare knows how to use on occasion. At the opposite extreme, before he averts the threat, he can carry it to the brink of tragedy, but always under control.

Dramatic irony is the result of a character or the audience anticipating an outcome which, comically or tragically, turns out very differently. Sometimes *we* foresee that it will. The speaker never foresees how ironical, looking back, the words or expectations will appear. When she says, 'A little water clears us of this deed,' Lady Macbeth has no prevision of her sleep-walking words, 'Will these hands ne'er be clean?' There is irony in the way in which in all Shakespeare's tragic plays except *Richard II* comedy is found in the very heart of the tragedy. The Porter scene in *Macbeth* comes straight after Duncan's murder. In *Hamlet* and *Antony and Cleopatra* comic episodes lead into the catastrophe: the rustic Countryman brings Cleopatra the means of death, and the satirised Osric departs with Hamlet's assent to the fatal fencing match. The Porter, the Countryman and Osric are not mere 'comic relief', they contrast with the tragedy in a way that adds something to it, and affects our response.

A sense of the comic and the tragic is common ground between Shakespeare and his audience. Understandings shared with the audience are necessary to all drama. They include conventions, i.e. assumptions, contrary to what factual realism would demand, which the audience silently agrees to accept. It is, after all, by a convention, what Coleridge called a 'willing suspension of disbelief', that an actor is accepted as Hamlet. We should let a play teach us the conventions it depends on. Shakespeare's conventions allow him to take a good many liberties, and he never troubles about inconsistencies that wouldn't trouble an audience. What matters to the dramatist is the effect he creates. So long as we are responding as he would wish, Shakespeare would not care whether we could say by what means he has made us do so. But to appreciate his skill, and get a fuller understanding of his play, we have to distinguish these means, and find terms to describe them.

If you approach the Shakespeare play you are studying bearing in mind what is said to you here, then you will respond to it more fully than before. Yet like all works of artistic genius, Shakespeare's can only be analysed so far. His drama and its poetry will always have about them something 'which into words no critic can digest'.

HAROLD BROOKS

ACKNOWLEDGEMENT

Cover illustration: *The Return of Othello* by Thomas Stothard. Photograph reproduced by courtesy of the Governors of the Royal Shakespeare Theatre.

NOTE   All references to act, scene and line numbering refer to the Macmillan Shakespeare edition of *Othello*, edited by Celia Hilton and R. T. Jones, but, as all references are clearly identified, this Master Guide may be used with any edition of the play.

1 LIFE AND BACKGROUND

1.1 LIFE

William Shakespeare was born in Stratford-upon-Avon, Warwick-shire, in 1564. We know only that he was christened in Holy Trinity church on 26 April but not the actual day of his birth, though it is widely accepted that it was 23 April, St. George's Day. Shakespeare's father was a prosperous glover and leather merchant, a man of property, who was mayor of Stratford in 1568. His fortunes declined from the mid 1570s, and he fell into debt and legal troubles.

It may be assumed that Shakespeare was educated at the local grammar school, although there is no record of him until his marriage to Anne Hathaway in November 1582. The following year his daughter, Susanna, was born, and in 1585 twins, Hamnet and Judith. Quite soon after this Shakespeare must have moved to London, for by 1592 he was already established as an actor and rising dramatist. We know this because in a pamphlet of that year the writer, Robert Greene, warned his fellow university-educated dramatists about 'This upstart Crow' of an actor who presumed to write plays, and who was 'in his own conceit the only Shake-scene in a country'. From quotations in Greene's pamphlet, it is evident that Shakespeare had already written the three *Henry VI* plays. Between 1592 and 1594 the theatres were closed because of outbreaks of plague in London, and during this time Shakespeare's two narrative poems, *Venus and Adonis* and *The Rape of Lucrece*, and probably many of his sonnets, were written.

By 1594 Shakespeare was a member of the successful company of actors known as the Lord Chamberlain's Men, who frequently performed before the Queen, and who became the King's Men under the patronage of her successor, James I. *Othello* was acted before him during the Christmas festivities of 1604. Shakespeare's fortunes rose in the 1590s. He became a very popular dramatist; he acquired a noble patron in the Earl of Southampton, to whom his narrative poems were dedicated; his family was granted a coat of arms in 1596, and in 1597 he bought New Place, a large house in Stratford; and he had a financial share in the enterprise when the Lord Chamberlain's Men moved to the newly-built Globe Theatre in 1599.

It was during the 1590s that Shakespeare wrote his English history plays, with the exception of *Henry VIII* (1613), and most of his romantic comedies. In 1599, he turned to Roman history with *Julius Caesar*, the first of a series of great tragedies. Earlier he had experimented with tragedy in *Titus Andronicus* (1594) and in *Romeo and Juliet* (1596), but the early 1600s are the years which produced the famous tragedies, *Hamlet* (1600–1), *Othello* (1604), *King Lear* (1605) and *Macbeth* (1606) and the 'problem' plays: *All's Well that Ends Well* (1602), *Troilus and Cressida* (1602) and *Measure for Measure* (1604). Shakespeare returned to Roman history with *Antony and Cleopatra* (1607) and *Coriolanus* (1608), before turning to write romantic tragicomedies in the last phase of his career, *Pericles* (1608), *Cymbeline* (1609), *The Winter's Tale* (1610) and *The Tempest* (1611), plays in which situations of potential tragedy are presented, but in which death and destruction are averted by supernatural or near-supernatural means so that the plays end with the restoration of harmony and a sense of renewed life.

Shakespeare's final years were spent in retirement at Stratford where he died in 1616. Seven years later, in 1623, his works were collected by two of his friends and members of the company, John Heminges and Henry Condell, and printed in what is known as the First Folio. During his lifetime about half of Shakespeare's plays appeared in print in what, because of their size, are called Quartos. *Othello* first appeared in a quarto edition in 1622. In the preface to the First Folio, Heminges and Condell write that their intention is to replace the many imperfect versions of Shakespeare's plays which had appeared in quarto form with texts which would keep Shakespeare's fame alive.

1.2 SHAKESPEARE'S TRAGEDIES

The use of the term 'Shakespearean tragedy' tends to obscure the fact that the tragic plays which the dramatist wrote are in many ways very different from each other. His two early experiments with the form, *Titus Andronicus* (1594) and *Romeo and Juliet* (1596) bear little resemblance to each other. The former is a play of bloodshed, violence and revenge, with sensational and horrific effects (one character has her tongue torn out and her hands chopped off after being raped; another unknowingly eats her two sons in a pie served at a banquet), and is set in ancient Rome. *Romeo and Juliet* is a tragedy of love set in Renaissance Italy. It bears many resemblances to the comedies which Shakespeare was writing at this time and has connections with Elizabethan love poetry, particularly the sonnet sequences. In 1599, with *Julius Caesar*, Shakespeare began to turn his attention more fully to writing tragedies, and *Hamlet*, *Othello*, *King Lear* and *Macbeth* followed closely upon each other. These plays show a considerable interest in character. Whereas Romeo and Juliet remain much the same throughout the play in which they appear, and their love is not undermined or destroyed, in the great Shakespearean tragedies of the early seventeenth century the central characters undergo a process of change, and the very qualities which made them heroic or noble are undermined during the course of the play. Yet not one of these plays is really like another, and it is difficult, even fallacious, to attempt to trace a development from one to the other. It seems almost incredible that after the bleakness, complexity and questioning of *King Lear*, Shakespeare wrote the compact and more direct tragedy of *Macbeth*. *Othello* is the only one of the four great tragedies to have love as its central concern and to have an essentially domestic setting. By its subject it is linked to the early tragedy of *Romeo and Juliet* and the later tragedy of *Antony and Cleopatra*, but the latter is played out on the stage of the political world, not in a domestic setting.

One way in which the diverse body of plays which make up Shakespeare's tragic writing may be seen to be connected is in their concern with a question which is central to tragedy as a genre, the question of the extent to which human beings have control over their lives and destinies. In *Romeo and Juliet* Shakespeare presents two 'star-cross'd lovers', as the Prologue to the play announces. Their fate is pre-determined, written in the stars. Throughout the play there are references in the text which suggest a fate at work outside the control of the human characters; for instance, Juliet has a premonition of death as she watches Romeo descend from her window after the night they have spent together. With the growing interest in character in the great tragedies comes a sense that in some respects character may be destiny, that the kind of person a man is may determine, or help to determine, what happens to him. These plays examine the interplay of external and internal (that is, character) forces at work in the tragic process, and each play presents a different analysis and places a different emphasis upon these forces. Hamlet may be viewed as a tragic victim; he does not initiate the tragic process by his own actions or decisions. His uncle, Claudius, has secretly murdered the king, Hamlet's father, and has taken his place both as ruler and as husband to Hamlet's mother. An external agency, the ghost of Hamlet's father, places upon Hamlet the task of avenging his death, a task to which, by reason of his character, he is unfitted. Hamlet is thus placed in a situation which is not of his own making. King Lear and Macbeth on the other hand are both responsible for the series of events which lead to their downfalls and the disintegration of their worlds. Character plays a great part in determining what happens to each of them. However, even these two plays are very different. King Lear is quite oblivious to the consequences of his actions at the beginning of the play, and the tragic process involves his coming to understand his own nature and the degree of his own responsibility for his suffering. Macbeth, on the other hand, sees clearly what the consequences of killing the king will be, but he still goes ahead and does the deed. For Lear the tragedy lies in his inability to know himself and to see what he is doing. For Macbeth the tragedy lies in the fact that he has understanding and moral insight and yet still pursues the course of action which will destroy him. There seems to be a great stress in *King Lear* on character as destiny. Although almost all the characters in the play refer to the gods, we are left with no sense that they exist, that there is a divine order, or at least that it has any interest in human affairs. Often it seems characters see the gods simply as projections of their own view of the world, and we are left with a feeling that it is human decisions and actions which determine the course of human life. In *Macbeth*, however, the presence of the Witches, the appearance of the ghost of Banquo, and the apparitions in the cavern scene suggest a supernatural dimension and indeed the play projects a strong sense of external evil. Initially Macbeth has freedom of choice whether to kill the king. The prophecy of the Witches may serve to stimulate the ambitious thoughts he already has, but it does not compel him to take the course of action he does. Once he has made the decision to kill the king, however, Macbeth is taken over by evil. He cannot escape from the consequences of his action and thus loses his ability to control his life. He has put himself into the power of evil forces and his doom is inevitable.

In *Othello*, the interplay of external and internal forces is different again. There is certainly an external force of evil which finds its embodiment in Iago. He uses the very qualities of good in Desdemona and Othello – her generosity of spirit and his trust in human honesty – to undermine them. However, as Chapter 3 will show there is no agreement among critics about how we should view Othello's character, and consequently no real agreement about the extent to which Othello's downfall results from the kind of man he is. Critics like F. R. Leavis who see Othello as self-concerned and self-dramatising suggest that he is greatly to blame for the tragic outcome. Other critics lay a greater stress upon Iago's responsibility for the destruction of Othello and Desdemona. Martin L. Wine in *Othello: Text and Performance* (see 'Further reading') says 'of Shakespeare's four great tragic heroes, Othello remains the least accessible to explanation and understanding' (Wine, p. 11). Though it may seem a simpler and more limited tragedy than *Hamlet* or *King Lear*, clearer in outline and more concentrated in terms of time scheme and number of characters, *Othello* presents us with considerable problems of interpretation, because Shakespeare's text allows a wide range of possibilities, particularly with regard to the characters of Othello himself and Iago. For purposes of clarity, the commentary in the second section of this Master Guide provides you with one possible interpretation of the play, but remember as you read that there are other possibilities. The range of interpretation allowed by the text might have been discussed in relation to each individual scene, but such a procedure would have made it difficult for you to form a clear view of the play as a whole. Later sections of this book, however, provide you with indications of the critical debate and of problems of interpretation, which should lead you to think more fully about the view provided by the Commentary. They should also lead you to reread the play itself, and, in doing so, to form your own views and interpretation.

2 SUMMARY AND CRITICAL COMMENTARY

Act I, Scene i

Summary

The play opens at night in a Venetian street outside the house of the senator, Brabantio. Roderigo, a young gentleman, complains that Iago, to whom he has apparently paid money for assistance in arranging a marriage with Brabantio's daughter, Desdemona, has not told him that she has secretly married Othello, the Moorish general. Iago tries to pacify Roderigo by expressing his own hatred for Othello, explaining that he has been passed over for the post of Othello's lieutenant in favour of the inexperienced Cassio. He tells Roderigo that the only reason he continues in Othello's service in the more lowly rank of ensign is that it may provide him with the opportunity to take revenge. Iago encourages Roderigo to rouse Brabantio and tell him about his daughter's elopement and marriage. Brabantio goes to summon help to search for Othello and Desdemona. Iago has meanwhile slipped away to rejoin his master in order to maintain an appearance of loyalty and faithfulness.

Commentary

The play opens in the middle of an interchange between Roderigo and Iago, so the audience only gradually forms an understanding of who the characters are and what is happening. Although it is evident that Roderigo is angry with Iago, who at first has difficulty in getting him to listen to his explanation (4), the audience does not gather the reason for this anger until the next part of the scene, in which Brabantio's speeches make clear that Roderigo has been a suitor for Desdemona, and Roderigo announces to her father that she has secretly married the Moor. What is immediately established is that Roderigo has a grievance against Iago, whom he has trusted even with his personal finances – 'thou. . . who hast had my purse/As if the strings were thine' (2–3). It is significant that the first moments of the play present us with a situation of apparent betrayal of trust between friends. Iago's lines,

> Now, sir, be judge yourself
> Whether I in any just term am affined
> To love the Moor! (38–40)

suggest that for some reason, as yet unrevealed, Roderigo thinks Iago has been withholding information from him for the Moor's advantage. The latter part of the scene presents another character, Brabantio, who also expresses feelings of betrayal, the betrayal of the trust he had in his daughter – 'Oh, she deceives me/Past thought' (166–7); 'Oh treason of the blood!/Fathers, from hence trust not your daughters' minds/By what you see them act' (170–2). The main tragic action of the play will focus upon Othello's sense of betrayed trust in Desdemona, so it is appropriate that the opening scene should concentrate so emphatically upon feelings of betrayal, thus announcing a major theme of the play. Iago's expression of anger at being passed over by Othello for the post of lieutenant may also be seen as the expression of feelings of betrayal. He presents the successful Cassio as a man who lacks experience of war and military matters, a theoretician ('a great arithmetician' (19)) who has read books on the subject and can talk about it but who has not, like Iago, actually been in a battle. Iago's words suggest feelings of betrayal in his relationship with his commander whose 'eyes had seen the proof' of his abilities in action, and who must have known how well Iago had served him. As a result of his dutiful service he could have expected to be promoted when the lieutenantship became vacant, but he suggests that promotion now seems to be a matter of influence and of personal whim on the part of the master. He scorns his position of 'ancient', or ensign, as if it were an insult.

We sense with all three characters in this scene that by being betrayed, or apparently betrayed, in these different ways, they also feel they have been made to look foolish. The reaction of Iago and Brabantio to this is to attack those who have hurt them. Later in the play Othello is tortured by the thought that not only has Desdemona been unfaithful but that, as a result, he has been made a cuckold, a figure of ridicule. Betrayal, or a sense of it, releases vindictive and destructive forces. Iago indicates that he continues to serve Othello only to serve himself and to exploit the situation for his own ends. It is clear that he himself will be prepared to betray his master's trust if it is to his advantage.

Roderigo's anger against Iago is skilfully deflected by the ensign on to Othello, who has taken the woman Roderigo himself wished to marry. Iago makes him feel that they are united in a common cause against the Moor.

As noted earlier, it is not until later in the scene that the audience knows the reason for Roderigo's complaints with which the play opens. Shakespeare quickly focuses the scene upon Iago's own grievances. It is these to which the dramatist gives initial prominence, and to the character of Iago, because they will be of central importance to the ensuing tragic action. The first scene provides the audience with a perspective on characters and events that is largely that of Iago. Othello himself does not appear but he is frequently mentioned, though not by name. Our first impressions of him are therefore those which derive from Iago. Just as we do not immediately know what Roderigo's grievances are, so we do not initially know who is the person referred to at line 7 simply as 'him'. Iago's following speech presents a picture of someone of considerable importance since even 'the great ones of the city' show him reverence, but who is full of pride and self-importance, and given to speaking in a bombastic manner. His choice of the supposedly inexperienced Cassio instead of the experienced Iago is presented as a matter of whim and suggests lack of good judgement. A distinctly unflattering portrait emerges, and is is noticeable that Othello is referred to finally only as 'the Moor', thus stressing his racial difference, a point which is underlined when Roderigo refers to him as 'the thick-lips' (66). When Iago tries to rouse Brabantio's anger, he uses animal imagery, referring to Othello as 'an old black ram' (88) and 'a Barbary horse' (112). He also associates him with the devil, when he tells Brabantio 'the devil will make a grandsire of you' (91). Iago's exaggeration even goes so far as to suggest that the physical union of Othello and Desdemona is bestial and will produce not human beings but animals – Brabantio will have 'coursers for cousins, and jennets for germans' (113–14). A particularly striking image comes in Iago's lines 'your daughter and the Moor are now making the beast with two backs' (116–18), a vulgar way of saying that they are having sexual intercourse. The image suggests something monstrous, and indeed the words 'monster' and 'monstrous' recur frequently during the play. The last line of Act I refers to Iago's plan as a 'monstrous birth' and central to the play is the image of jealousy as 'the green-eyed monster, which doth mock/The meat it feeds on' (III, iii, 164–5).

It is not until the second scene that the audience is able to form a direct impression of Othello from his words and actions. The first scene, however, provides many signs that the view of Othello which is presented here should be regarded with some scepticism until there is fuller evidence. We are aware that Iago is a man with a grievance against, and indeed a hatred for, Othello, so we should be careful not to assume that his description of him is objective and to be trusted. The same also holds true of his denigratory portrait of Cassio, though that is of less importance in the scene as a whole. Moreover, what is established early in the first scene is Iago's own nature. His speech beginning at line 41 clearly shows that he is a character who is not to be trusted. He is not one of those who dutifully serve their masters in a self-abnegating manner, but like those

> Who, trimmed in forms and visages of duty,
> Keep yet their hearts attending on themselves,
> And throwing but shows of service on their lords
> Do well thrive by them; . . . (50–3)

He ends 'I am not what I am' (65). Iago cultivates a deceptive appearance of service and loyalty in order to serve his own ends. We find frequently in Shakespeare's plays that evil is characterised by just this disjunction between outward appearance and inner reality. Later in the scene we are reminded again of Iago's deceptive nature: as Brabantio goes in, Iago slips away to join Othello, telling Roderigo:

> Though I do hate him as I do hell pains,
> Yet for necessity of present life
> I must show out a flag and sign of love,
> Which is indeed but sign. (155–8)

If indeed he is a person whose outward appearance and actions are not to be trusted, then we cannot be sure that anything he says or does when others are present should be taken at face value. The first scene provides indications of Iago's manipulative activity. It is he who suggests the plan to rouse Brabantio and who instructs his companion how to go about it, so that it will appear to be done on Roderigo's initiative. When Brabantio appears it is noticeable that Roderigo is deferential and likely to be too indirect to communicate his message before Brabantio sends him off as a mere trouble-maker. Roderigo's speeches are very short in the first part of the exchange with Brabantio and indicate both politeness – 'Signior . . . most reverend signior . . . Sir . . . good sir . . . Most grave Brabantio' – and difficulty in making Desdemona's father listen to him: 'Sir, sir, sir . . . Patience, good sir.' It is Iago who interjects coarse, indeed obscene, and direct statements and images which are calculated to outrage Brabantio: first, when Roderigo is insufficiently forthright, 'Even now, now, very now, an old black ram/Is tupping your white ewe' (88–89), and secondly to make Brabantio listen when Roderigo is in danger of being sent packing without being able to tell the news, 'Zounds, sir, you are one of those that will not serve God if the devil bid you! Because we come to do you service, and you think we are ruffians, you'll have your daughter covered with a Barbary horse' (108–12). We are given here in little an example of how Iago will work on Othello to make him jealous. His words and the images he uses are calculated to have a disturbing emotional impact, thus releasing powerful destructive forces of anger and vengeance. For Brabantio Iago evokes images of the sexual union of Othello and Desdemona which forcefully establish contrasts between the young, innocent girl and the Moor. The presentation of human sexual intercourse as if it were the copulation of animals would establish in Brabantio a sharp sense of defilement of his daughter's purity. The animal images are important in the play and it is appropriate that they appear in this form here at the opening. When we see Othello in the second scene his humanity and nobility are in direct contrast to the degrading impression conveyed by Iago's description here. However, Iago's destructive plan aims to destroy just those noble human qualities and to reduce Othello to the state of a wild beast.

Just before they rouse Brabantio, Iago states his determination to undermine Othello's joy in his marriage, to 'poison his delight' (68) and to 'throw such chances of vexation on't,/As it may lose some colour' (72–3). There seems here to be an acknowledgement that the love of Othello and Desdemona is one of great happiness and fulfilment and is not the lustful, indulgent and bestial union which only a few minutes later he suggests to Brabantio. Iago is determined to undermine that happiness and peace of mind. The image of poison which occurs in this connection is important. Iago is associated with the debilitating and destructive action of poison here and elsewhere in the play, for example II. iii. 367. At this stage Iago does not seem to consider that he is able to destroy Othello's happiness but only to detract from it by raising these troubles. A little later he admits that Brabantio will not bring Othello down because the state needs him in the Cyprus war. The play will show how Iago's plans for vexation and for the undermining of joy become more ambitious and destructive, and how Othello becomes more vulnerable. The first scene provides the basis of our understanding of the origins of the later developments: it establishes Iago as a character and it announces central themes and images. It is also significant in being a night scene. A large number of scenes in the play take place at night. If we take the storm in II. i, as, if not actually taking place at night, providing an overshadowing of the normal light of day, it is not until the beginning of Act III that there is a daylight scene, and in IV. iii, day is drawing to a close, while the whole of the final act takes place at night. (Section 3.1.2 below deals with the light/darkness contrasts.)

Act I, Scene ii

Summary
Iago has told Othello that Brabantio knows of Desdemona's elopement. He pretends that he had restrained himself with difficulty from

killing Roderigo for maligning Othello. Cassio arrives with others to summon Othello to the Senate on urgent business. Brabantio, Roderigo and officers then arrive. Othello restrains those present from fighting, and when Brabantio wants to lead him to prison, Othello tells him of the Duke's summons. Brabantio decides to go with Othello to seek redress from the senators for the wrong he has suffered in the loss of his daughter.

Commentary
The ability of Iago to assume a deceptive appearance is demonstrated at the opening of this scene. Having in the previous scene expressed hatred for Othello, and stirred up Brabantio against him, using obscene and degrading comparisons, he now makes a show of loyalty to his master. It is obvious that the blame for making trouble with Desdemona's father has been laid on Roderigo, and indeed Iago ascribes to him the insulting descriptions of Othello which he himself has made. If Iago is here trying to inflame Othello's anger against Roderigo and to make conflict more likely when Brabantio arrives, he does not succeed. What is most striking is Othello's calmness, confidence and dignity. Indeed we are presented with a very different man from the one described in the first scene of the play. He is not vindictive; he says that it is better that Iago did not kill Roderigo (6), and threats and insults do not touch him for he is sure that they will be ineffectual and seen as untrue. He is confident that his own worth, nobility and the truth of his love for Desdemona will be evident. The state knows his worth from his former services; he is of noble birth – 'I fetch my life and being/From men of royal siege'; and his love for Desdemona is sure, as he says he would not have given up his independence lightly. Though there is pride here, it is not the kind of pride suggested by Iago's speech in I. i, 8–17 – 'loving his own pride and purposes' – which suggests a man who is arrogant, boastful, temperamental and erratic in his judgement. What we see in the second scene is a man who has a rightful pride in himself that has nothing to do with arrogance and inflated ego, but with a sense of true worth. Indeed, he rejects boasting as dishonourable (20) and he says that his present position was reached as a just desert for his actions which may be spoken of modestly, just as they were, with no need to elaborate or inflate them (22–4).

As lights are seen, Iago assumes that it must be Brabantio and his followers, and advises Othello to go in. Such an action might have appeared to indicate bad conscience, or a desire to hide, but Othello's nobility and confidence in the rightness of what he has done make him shun such advice and remain to meet Desdemona's father. His speech (30–2) shows that he feels he has nothing to hide – 'My parts, my title, and my perfect soul/Shall manifest me rightly.' This honesty and openness stand in direct contrast to the deviousness and deception of Iago, and our attention is drawn to the fact by his oath,

'By Janus', who was, appropriately, a two-faced Roman god. Othello's words and behaviour establish him as a man of complete integrity in whom there is a correspondence between the inner reality of his nature and his outward appearance.

The audience anticipates the arrival of Brabantio who had been summoning his followers at the end of the previous scene, so that, like Iago, we expect the approaching torches to be theirs. Shakespeare does not immediately satisfy our expectations, and thus maintains tension as the threatened confrontation is still to come. He also makes the audience interested to know the reason for the arrival of the unexpected band of men. Cassio summons Othello to the Venetian council. His speech indicates urgent activity in the night; he speaks of the 'dozen sequent messengers' who have arrived at Venice 'at one another's heels' with news of the Cyprus wars, and he tells how groups have been searching the city for Othello as he could not be found at his usual lodgings. The comings and goings indicated in the speech reinforce the sense of agitation and activity in the night conveyed by the action of this scene itself, with the arrival first of Cassio's band of men with torches, then of Brabantio and his followers, and, finally, with all of them going to the Senate. Cassio's speech also suggests to us a correspondence between the impending threat to the state which the arrival of the messengers and the emergency meeting of the council indicate, and the threat to Othello's personal life posed by the imminent and expected arrival of Brabantio.

Othello's behaviour when Brabantio does arrive confirms our impression of his calmness, confidence and nobility. Iago draws his sword and threatens to attack Roderigo, but is stopped by Othello. He further attempts to calm the situation by saying that Brabantio has no need to attempt to enforce his will by means of weapons, since Othello respects the authority which his age gives him – 'you shall more commend with years/Than with your weapons' (60–1).

In contrast to Othello's calmness, dignity and politeness, Brabantio is impassioned and insulting. He twice calls Othello a thief and accuses him of using magic to bewitch his daughter. He cannot understand how otherwise Desdemona, who showed no interest in marriage to young Venetians, could be attracted to black Othello, and for Brabantio the only explanation must be that he had used magic charms on her. Brabantio's sense of Othello's otherness is very strong here, and at the end of the scene he states that if the Senate gives approval to the match between the Moor and Desdemona, the result will be that the Venetian state will be ruled by 'Bond slaves and pagans'. The remark implicitly stresses that Othello is not a white, Christian Venetian. Though it is clear from the play that he is a convert to Christianity, attention is drawn to his pagan origins by Brabantio to make his charge of witchcraft the more credible. For seventeenth-century Englishmen black was the devil's colour, and paganism was associated with magic and practices which were devilish. Brabantio thus accuses Othello of underhand dealings, of practising forbidden arts, a charge which is at variance with the openness, honesty and nobility of Othello's actions and words in this scene. The Othello of Brabantio's imagination is like Iago's Othello in the first scene which we see now clearly to be false. The Moor remains calm in the face of these accusations and insults, and again commands those present not to fight. He says that he would have fought if this had been a fighting matter in which it would have been dishonourable not to fight. Thus the scene presents us with a number of important contrasts which focus upon Othello himself – contrasts between Othello as he is described in the first scene and as he appears here, between Iago's deviousness and Othello's integrity, between the Moor's dignity and calmness and Brabantio's undignified and insulting behaviour. The scene also suggests a correspondence between public and private events in terms of threat and danger for which Othello is the focus. The coming together of public and private is anticipated at the end of the scene as all the characters go the Senate.

Act I, Scene iii

Summary
The Senate receives conflicting reports of the numbers and intentions of the enemy Turks. Finally it seems certain that they intend to attack Cyprus. At this point Othello, Brabantio and their followers arrive. The Duke listens to Brabantio's complaints and then hears Othello. Desdemona is sent for and verifies his version of events. The Senate then resumes discussions of the political situation. Othello is to be sent as governor to Cyprus. Desdemona is allowed to accompany him, though in another ship in Iago's charge. Roderigo is in despair because his hopes of marrying Desdemona have been dashed. Iago persuades him that she will tire of Othello and will look for a lover. The scene ends with a soliloquy from Iago who indicates he is merely using Roderigo. He lights upon the idea of using Cassio to make Othello jealous.

Commentary
The scene opens with the Senate discussing conflicting reports of Turkish numbers. As the Duke's first lines indicate, the senators do not know what to believe. However, even if the numbers are uncertain, he agrees with the Second Senator that all the reports seem to indicate that a Turkish fleet is heading for Cyprus. At that moment a sailor enters with news that the Turks are making for Rhodes, thus adding to the uncertainty by putting in question the one sure point

which all the former reports had seemed to indicate. The First Senator suggests that the latest Turkish move is a deception — 'a pageant/To keep us in false gaze' (18–19) — to hide the enemy's real intention to attack Cyprus. A messenger then arrives with news which confirms this assessment of the situation. The opening of this scene, therefore, shows that the upheaval in the personal lives of Othello, Desdemona and Brabantio is taking place against a background of threatening and uncertain events. This adds to the tension and the hurried arrivals of the Sailor and the Messenger, one after the other, convey a sense of fast moving events.

The public matters presented here are not unrelated to the matter of the previous two scenes. The Senate in the third scene is like the audience in the previous ones, trying to assess the truth of words and actions, whilst the Turks, with their ploy of appearing to be about to attack Rhodes when their actual intention is to attack Cyprus, provide us with an example of deceptive appearance used to gain advantage in the public world, as Iago uses it in the private world of the play. The implied correspondence between Iago and the enemies of Christianity, or true faith, as the audience of the time would have seen it, is one of the ways in which Shakespeare defines Iago's evil and associates it with the wider working of evil within the world. As he seeks to destroy the relationship of Othello and Desdemona by undermining the faith on which it is based, the Turks seek to destroy Christendom.

The arrival of Othello and Brabantio precipitates another crisis for the Senate when it is discovered that the apparent seducer of Desdemona, whom the Duke vows to punish even if he were his own son, is none other than the man of whom they have most need in the present political situation. The next part of the scene provides another example of people trying to understand the truth of a situation from the various reports of it which they are given. Othello is allowed to speak in his defence, and the Duke shows a determination to obtain proof: He dismisses Brabantio's argument that Desdemona could only have fallen in love with Othello through the operation of witchcraft by saying that assertions such as this are no proof (106–9). The scene thus develops into a trial, which Othello presents as a trial of his integrity. He immediately admits that he has taken Desdemona from her father and has married her (78–9), further confirming the impression of openness and honesty which we noted in the second scene. He asks the Duke to send for Desdemona so that she may testify, and he suggests that for him to lie to the Senate in this matter would forfeit the trust they might have in him in other matters. The betrayal of trust, or assumed betrayal, is a major concern of the play.

Othello's defence and explanation to the Senate is the opportunity for Shakespeare to provide the audience with information about events which have occurred before the play opens and to deepen understanding of Othello's character. He speaks calmly and respectfully to his masters — 'Most potent, grave and reverend signiors' – in a style which is again in contrast to the rather intemperate nature of Brabantio's speeches. Although Othello modestly says 'Rude am I in my speech' (81), his speech is actually eloquent, but it is an eloquence which does not disguise or hide the truth but makes us and the Senate more fully aware of it. He says he will tell a 'round unvarnished tale', suggesting that he will tell things as they were. What his eloquence does is to create a sense of a man who, through his ability to tell in a vivid and interesting manner the story of his colourful and adventurous life, could easily have attracted Desdemona. The audience listens enrapt to the speeches, and the Duke's comment, 'I think this tale would win my daughter too' (170), testifies to the way in which their style and manner have actually been the means of revealing the truth because they convince the listeners that Desdemona could have fallen in love with this man.

The speeches establish Othello as a man whose life has been spent in military action (83–6), which has taken him to distant and exotic places and has involved him in many adventures. Both the style and content of these speeches establish Othello as very different from the people to whom he speaks. This difference, which is a strength or advantage here, will also be used later by Iago in the process of making him jealous.

Othello's words, 'Her father loved me; oft invited me;/Still questioned me the story of my life', place Brabantio in a rather unfavourable light as they are in direct contrast to his present behaviour. It seems he was perfectly happy to have such an exotic and interesting guest and showed considerable liking for him, but liking turns to loathing when this same man becomes his son-in-law.

Othello's speech also provides important information about Desdemona before her appearance. Until this point the audience has received little impression of her beyond the fact that she is young and is Brabantio's daughter. Othello tells how, while he would relate his adventures to her father, Desdemona would come to listen in between dealing with household affairs. This is an interesting detail. Desdemona is clearly not a young lady of leisure who has nothing to do but have romantic daydreams. We hear nothing of her mother, and Shakespeare may well be implying that she is dead and that Desdemona had the managing of the domestic affairs of her father's household. Such responsibility and authority might indeed have given her the maturity and confidence which she later displays in this scene. This detail helps to prevent us from gaining the impression that she was the sort of immature and empty-headed girl who might easily have been carried away with the apparent glamour of Othello and his exotic adventures. Othello himself also makes clear that Desdemona herself had taken initiatives in the wooing (162–5). His words do not suggest a shy, retiring girl. Though they do not show her overstepping the limits of social propriety, they indicate a young woman who is capable of taking initiatives and having some control over her life. Othello ends his speech by refuting Brabantio's charge of witchcraft. No charms and potions have been used, only the magic of human affections and reciprocal love (168).

Shakespeare has left the appearance of his third major character, Desdemona, until this late moment, and it is she who finally confirms the truth of what Othello has said. This is part of very careful dramatic structuring; the first scene establishes Iago as a character, the second focuses upon Othello, and the third, whilst revealing more about Othello, also introduces Desdemona. Additionally, the three scenes of the first act provide all we need to know in terms of exposition, but Shakespeare reveals the information gradually so that we are kept in expectation and a questioning frame of mind until the latter part of the third scene, when we finally have a complete picture.

Desdemona's behaviour is exemplary. She speaks respectfully to her father, but the sureness of her love for Othello is evident in the confidence with which she states publicly that her primary duty is towards her husband. She is neither overawed by her father nor by being called to the ducal council. She speaks up when she is told that Othello must go to Cyprus, requesting that she may go with him. She says that she loves Othello for his virtues and she talks of consecrating her 'soul and fortunes' to him. The words suggest a spiritual basis to the relationship, but this is complemented by an indication of an equally strong physical dimension as she argues that if Othello goes to Cyprus and she is left behind, 'the rites for why I love him are bereft me' (254). The speech suggests a complete and balanced love relationship, quite different from Iago's suggestions in the first scene and later in this of one based simply on physical attraction and lust. Othello too assures the senators that, if they allow his wife to accompany him, he is capable of exercising responsible control so that his personal life does not affect the performance of his public duties.

By this point the exposition is complete. As Othello leaves to go to Cyprus, Shakespeare introduces ominous and ironic moments which prepare us for the ensuing tragedy. First, Othello puts Desdemona into Iago's safe-keeping, saying of him 'A man he is of honesty and trust' (281), and calling him 'Honest Iago' (291). The audience is aware how misplaced is this trust and of the dangers that might ensue. Secondly, the Duke's words to Brabantio, 'Your son-in-law is far more fair than black' (287), draws attention to deceptive appearances and helps to underline that Iago's fair-seeming hides inner evil. Thirdly, Brabantio's farewell to Othello provides a warning which will be echoed in III. 3. 204, when Iago reminds Othello of it. Othello in response to Brabantio affirms his faith in his wife in words heavy with dramatic irony, 'My life upon her faith' (291).

The scene then changes appropriately from verse to prose for the expression of Roderigo's foolish despair and Iago's cynical view of life. Roderigo has no resourcefulness and thinks that all his hopes of gaining Desdemona are lost. To convince him otherwise Iago presents a view of the relationship of Othello and his wife as merely physical, and of human nature as changeable, telling Roderigo that therefore the marriage cannot last long. For him love is merely lust. There is no acknowledgement of human dignity or virtues and his refrain 'Put money in thy purse', emphasises the materialistic and cynical view of life which is expressed here to persuade Roderigo. He convinces him that they are united in their desire for revenge on Othello.

The scene ends with a soliloquy from Iago, which, since it is spoken to no one else, may be taken to be an expression of his genuine thoughts. He is scornful of Roderigo and indicates that he is simply using him. He again expresses his hatred for Othello but this time introduces another motive for revenge, a rumour that the Moor had committed adultery with Iago's wife (386–8). He has no proof of it but is jealous enough to want revenge. The irrationality of his feelings is clear when later in the speech he admits that Othello has 'a free and open nature', thus acknowledging that he is not the sort of man who would deceive in this or any other way. Moreover, he has had plenty of evidence of Othello's honesty in his dealings with Brabantio and the Senate. The plan which Iago lights upon involves reducing Othello to that very state of jealousy which he himself feels. He will use the facts that Othello trusts him, that Cassio's attractiveness and courteousness make him easy to present as a likely lover, and that, because of his own integrity, Othello has no awareness of others' lack of it. The latter point Iago identifies as Othello's weakness; his very virtue makes him vulnerable. The soliloquy ends with words which sound diabolic. Iago's plan needs the assistance of the forces of evil and darkness – 'Hell and night' – and the sexual imagery suggests that he is conceiving a fearful monster. Brabantio had accused Othello of witchcraft, but the final lines of the scene suggest that it is Iago who is associated with such practices.

Act II, Scene i

Summary
The action moves to Cyprus where a sea storm is raging. News arrives that the Turkish fleet is scattered and that Cassio's ship has arrived from Venice. The ship bearing Iago, Desdemona and Emilia puts into port soon after. A trumpet announces the arrival of Othello, who

is reunited with his wife. Iago, left alone with Roderigo, tells him that Desdemona is in love with Cassio. Though at first he is sceptical, Roderigo agrees to go along with Iago's plan to stir up trouble by provoking Cassio to a fight. The scene ends with a soliloquy from Iago, showing how his plan of revenge is beginning to take shape.

Commentary

In the early seventeenth-century theatre the action of the play would have been continuous, and we shall lose a full understanding of Shakespeare's dramatic effects if we allow act and scene divisions in the text to make us view each scene as a separate entity unrelated to what precedes or follows it. The storm which opens Act II comes immediately after Iago's words 'Hell and night/Must bring this monstrous birth to the world's light', and the effect of this juxtaposition is almost to suggest that the storm has been conjured up by him; indeed, it was believed at the time that storms might be raised by witchcraft. Though this is not literally the case, as Iago is not presented as a character with magical powers, the storm which heralds the arrival of Othello and Desdemona in Cyprus, where their tragedy will be played out, acts as a dramatic symbol of the evil and destructive conflicts which Iago is releasing.

Cassio, who had been mentioned in I. i, and who had a small part to play in I. ii, begins here to become more fully developed as a character. His 'smooth dispose' or courtly manner to which Iago refers (I. iii, 397) is shown at several points in the scene. His praise of Desdemona (61–5) is high indeed; he says that her beauty and person exceed what any poet or artist is capable of expressing, and his following lines (68–73) remind us of Elizabethan love poetry in which the perfection of the lady enables the lover to perceive the divine, and is capable even of affecting the workings of nature – the storm, the seas, the winds, rocks and sands respond to her beauty and cease to be dangerous, allowing her to pass safely. There may well be the suggestion in these lines that Cassio does indeed love Desdemona, his praise is so heartfelt and passionate, and so like that of an Elizabethan poet-lover. His poetic description of her journey in which she could not possibly come to harm helps to highlight for us by contrast the very real dangers that lie in wait for her as a result of the storm that Iago is creating. Later Iago shows how he will use the very goodness of her nature to destroy her (II. iii, 369–73). Cassio's description also stands in stark contrast to Iago's cynical view of women in the part of the scene immediately following, where he first criticises his wife for nagging, and then goes on to generalise unfavourably about women. When Desdemona asks how he would praise her he has, or pretends to have, difficulty. It is significant in relation to Cassio's earlier words that Iago presents himself as if he were a poet writing of a lady — 'my Muse labours' (127). Emilia had also said 'You shall not write my praise' (116). What Iago produces is a lame couplet:

> If she be fair and wise – fairness and wit,
> The one's for use, the other useth it. (129–30)

When Desdemona asks how he would praise a deserving woman (and we may see Desdemona herself as a woman who indeed deserves praise) Iago produces further empty couplets, containing not words of praise, but perhaps coarse, even obscene, suggestion (154), and ending in bathos and mockery

> She was a wight (if ever such wights were) – . . .
> To suckle fools and chronicle small beer. (157–9)

He had said earlier to Desdemona, 'I am nothing if not critical', and this dialogue proves him to be full of cynicism, unable to praise and lacking respect for women.

Iago's sentiments, however, are expressed in a bluff and hearty manner as if they were intended to make his hearers laugh, and this outward appearance of pleasantry provides a stark contrast to the reality of the inner malice he harbours, which is expressed in an aside as he watches Cassio conversing with Desdemona in a courtly, refined manner, very different from his own. He sees how he can use this very courtliness to destroy Cassio, and he uses imagery of entrapment – 'With as little a web as this will I ensnare as great a fly as Cassio' (167–8). The innocent and courteous gesture of taking Desdemona by the hand will be turned into something suspicious and devious. Shakespeare underlines that, for all Cassio's devotion to Desdemona, his behaviour here is quite innocent and simply courtesy by making Roderigo later in the scene rebut Iago's insinuations that it was an indication of lechery (257). Iago's aside ends with obscene suggestion (clyster pipes were tubes used for injection). Whilst the aside stands in contrast to his hearty manner in the preceding dialogue, it also stands in stark contrast to what follows immediately with Othello's entrance. The prose of Iago's aside changes to the majestic blank verse of the reunion of Othello and Desdemona. The language and the style move us on to a higher plane, and, indeed, Shakespeare draws our attention to the poetry, the 'music' of this moment, by giving Iago an aside, 'Oh, you are well tuned now!/But I'll set down the pegs that make this music' (197–8). The speeches of Othello and Desdemona contain a series of words which emphasise the harmony and joy of this moment – 'content' (repeated three times), 'joy' (twice), 'happy', 'loves', 'comforts'. Added to this is the sense of wonder expressed in lines 181–2. The totality of their love is expressed through references to soul; Othello calls Desdemona his 'soul's joy', and says

> My soul hath her content so absolute
> That not another comfort like to this
> Succeeds in unknown fate.

Such references indicate that this love is not as Iago would present it, a lust of the flesh, but one affecting the whole of their being. The references to soul and their prayers to the heavens and 'sweet Powers' show both reverence and a sense of love connected with the divine order.

The moment of reunion is an intense moment of stillness, harmony and perfection, but we are also aware of its transitoriness and of the vulnerable situation of the lovers through juxtaposition with Iago's threatening aside and by references within Othello's own speech. The image of the ship climbing 'hills of seas' and then ducking again 'as low/As hell's from heaven' (186–7) prefigures the fall of Othello from the divine perfection of this moment into a hell of jealousy. The peak of their fortunes has been reached and they will not long remain so happy as the dramatic irony of the following lines, 'If it were now to die,/'Twere now to be most happy', indicates.

At the end of the scene Iago suggests to Roderigo, as he did in the previous scene, that Desdemona is changeable, and he now states that she has already fallen in love with Cassio. He presents her relationship with Othello as a matter simply of physical attraction. Roderigo is not credulous, and now himself adds to the praise of Desdemona, whom he describes as 'full of most blessed condition', thus adding to the number of references within the scene which have connected her with the divine. However, despite his doubts of the truth of Iago's statements, Roderigo is weak enough to agree to the plan to provoke Cassio to a fight.

The concluding soliloquy shows how Iago's plan is emerging. The speech contains a notable acknowledgement that Othello 'Is of a constant, loving, noble nature' (293), which is very different from the assessment of his nature given to Roderigo earlier, 'These Moors are changeable in their wills' (I. iii, 348–9). This shows what he really believes, as it is spoken with no one else present, and yet again, as in the soliloquy at the end of the previous scene, he can irrationally talk of the same man as the 'lusty Moor' whom he suspects of committing adultery with Emilia. The emphasis in this soliloquy on sexual jealousy as a motivating factor for Iago is strong. We now have the additional indication that he is jealous of Cassio too (311), and the imagery of poison recurs here as Iago describes jealousy 'like a poisonous mineral' gnawing away within him. Tormented thus, he wishes to inflict upon Othello the same torment. Believing his own wife to be unfaithful, Iago wishes to destroy the constant, loving and trusting nature of the Othello–Desdemona relationship. His surprising statement that he too loves Desdemona (295) is another way of indicating his desire to sully Desdemona and to make her like his own wife as he believes her to be. It is noticeable that in this soliloquy as in the last Iago expresses the idea of making Othello an ass (I. iii, 401–2, II. i, 312–13). Whilst the image indicates the desire to make Othello an object of ridicule, it also indicates a desire to reduce this noble and honest man to an animal state, as in his descriptions in the first scene Iago reduces Othello to a ram and to a Barbary horse.

Act II, Scene ii

Summary
A herald announces the destruction of the Turkish fleet. Orders are given that the people should celebrate not only the enemy's defeat but Othello's marriage.

Commentary
Coming immediately after Iago's soliloquy this apparently unimportant brief scene has the dramatic effect of heightening our awareness of the threat to Othello and Desdemona, and of their total unawareness of it just at the moment when the first stage of Iago's plan is to be put into operation. The proclamation suggests that all is well now that the Turks have been defeated. The enemy within, however, is at work. It is not by chance that Shakespeare has already made us see connections between Iago and the Turks (I. iii – see Commentary on the opening section; II. i, 113).

Act II, Scene iii

Summary
Cassio is given responsibility for ensuring that the public celebrations do not get out of hand, but, with encouragement from Iago, he becomes drunk. Cassio beats Roderigo who has provoked him in accordance with Iago's prearranged plan. A fight ensues in which Montano is wounded. Othello is roused, and when he hears what has happened, he dismisses Cassio as his officer. Iago persuades the dismissed man to ask Desdemona to intercede with her husband on his behalf. Meanwhile Iago intends to make Othello think that his wife's concern for Cassio arises from secret love for him.

Commentary
Ironic effect is continued in the opening of this scene as Cassio assures Othello that Iago has everything under control so that the

celebrations do not get out of hand. We know that in fact he intends to manipulate the situation so that they do. Ironically, too, Othello as he retires to bed says that Iago is most trustworthy, thus strengthening the effect of the previous short scene by underlining his total unawareness of the evil which threatens, and showing him in a state of false security.

The following dialogue between Iago and Cassio presents contrasting views of Desdemona. The former is prurient in his comments, thinking of her physical attractiveness and lovemaking; he imagines Othello 'making wanton the night with her' (16); she is 'sport for Jove' (17), as beautiful as the human women with whom the god, Jupiter, fell in love in many ancient myths, recounted in the erotic tales of Ovid's *Metamorphoses*, which had been translated from Latin into English and were very popular in Shakespeare's time; she is 'full of game' (19) and has an enticing look (21–2). In contrast Cassio shows admiration and respect for her as a pure and innocent creature; she is 'most exquisite' (18), 'fresh and delicate' (20), 'right modest' (23), and 'indeed perfection' (28). If Cassio is in love with Desdemona, albeit from afar, as Iago believes he may be, the ensign's forcing upon him of mental pictures of her physical lovemaking which is continued with his line 'happiness to their sheets', would be very emotionally disturbing, and Iago, as he does with Brabantio earlier and Othello later, may well be seeking to provoke strong emotions in order to cause his victim to lose his self-control, in this case to make Cassio give in to an inclination to drown his sorrows in drink. Ironically, he is at first unsuccessful and it is Montano and the gentlemen who quite innocently persuade the lieutenant to drink, thus unwittingly furthering Iago's plan. He encourages the celebratory spirit by singing drinking songs and Cassio becomes drunk.

Iago's dialogue with Montano shows how he is capable of convincing others that a falsehood is a truth. Montano does not know Cassio, and so Iago is able to give a false report of him as a drunkard, unworthy of Othello's trust. Montano's statement that Othello should be told of Cassio's vice,

> Perhaps he sees it not, or his good nature
> Prizes the virtue that appears in Cassio
> And looks not on his evils. . . .   (137–9)

shows that Iago has been successful in convincing the former governor of Cyprus that Cassio is a person of deceptive appearance who should not be trusted, when in fact that person is Iago himself, who pretends he is a friend of Cassio and would not wish to speak ill of him to Othello.

The first two acts of *Othello* are full of movement and activity. The fight in this scene provides another moment of tense and exciting action, but it also provides an important visual image, to which Othello's words draw our attention. The previous scene had suggested the return of peace and security, whilst at the opening of this scene Othello had stressed the importance of good order and control. In this he shows his sense of responsibility; the celebration of his wedding night will not be the occasion for laxity, as he promised the Senate his personal life would not interfere with his public duties as governor of Cyprus. However, by the middle of the scene public order has been disturbed and Othello asks, 'Are we turned Turks, and to ourselves do that/Which heaven hath forbid the Ottomites?' (174–5), and he refers to 'this barbarous brawl' (176). The lines imply contrasts between Turks and Christians, enemies and friends, barbarism and civilisation. Othello asks if the Christian Venetians have become like the Turks the enemies of the state, and if, having by divine providence been saved from death at the hands of those enemies, they would now kill each other. This kind of disorder and quarrelling, he implies, is what might be expected of infidels and barbarians but not of Christians and civilised men. The visual image of the brawl is thus established as an image not simply of disorder but of self-destruction. The Turks may have been defeated but the values and attitudes they represent are still present, and, as the audience alone knows, primarily in Iago, between whom and the Turks the play has already made connections. Othello's exclamation about the brawl, '''Tis monstrous', reminds us Iago's 'monstrous birth' (I, iii, 404), his plot, which hell and night are inducing. Again ironically, Othello turns to Iago to learn the truth, calling him 'Honest Iago' (181), unaware that it is he who has fomented this situation. Othello speaks and acts here with a voice of authority and command but for the first time we see that beneath the outward composure and control he is capable of powerful emotions. When neither Cassio nor Montano will give an account of what happened, he becomes angry (208–11). It is important that Shakespeare reveals to us here that Othello is actually a man of powerful emotions which are capable of threatening his calm, controlled and reasonable manner, as this helps to make more credible the way in which the emotion of jealousy obliterates rationality later in the play. The change from the composure of Othello in the first act to the impassioned man of the fourth would have been difficult to accept without the insight we gain here.

Iago's show of reluctance at having to speak against Cassio and of trying to mitigate the offence that has been committed further confirms Othello's belief in his 'honesty' and 'love'. Indeed, throughout this scene he gives the appearance of being friendlily disposed towards Cassio. His later soliloquy reflects upon the way in which he uses the appearance of goodness to promote his evils.

Desdemona's brief appearance emphasises that the brawl has not only disturbed public order but the peace and harmony of the wedding night. It has separated Othello and Desdemona, momentarily, but Iago's earlier speech makes the brawl prefigure the conflict which will divide the lovers when he describes the fighters as

> Friends all, but now, even now;
> In quarter and in terms like bride and groom
> Devesting them for bed; and then, but now –
> .   .   .   .
>
> .   .   .   .
> In opposition bloody. (183–5, 188)

When Iago and Cassio are left alone the dialogue, like the earlier one about Desdemona, highlights their differences. Cassio is more concerned with moral matters, with reputation, at which Iago scoffs, suggesting that the only kind of hurts to worry about are physical ones. Cassio is concerned with personal integrity, with there being a correspondence between the nature of the man and the public report of him. Good reputation is 'the immortal part' of himself because it is what makes a man remembered after his death. He will now be known as a drunkard, a man unable to control himself, who allows his emotions and physical nature to overcome his reason. He says that in so doing he has made himself no better than a beast (268, 299), and that it is the devil, wine, and the devil, anger, that have reduced him to this state; but the audience knows that it is another devil, Iago, who has been the instigator of all this, and in his soliloquy which follows he does in fact identify himself as a devil (362–5). In it he shows that he knows Desdemona to be a woman who is generous and compassionate who will want to help Cassio. Her very goodness will be the means by which he will destroy them. Imagery of poison recurs as Iago speaks of pouring 'pestilence' into Othello's ear by making him believe that Desdemona is in love with Cassio because she pleads so strongly for him. Just as he wants to transform the noble Moor into an ass, he wishes, in Othello's mind at least, to transform Desdemona's virtue 'into pitch', to make what is fair seem foul. The scene ends with Iago seeing how he needs to develop his plan using his wife, Emilia. His manipulation of characters and events in the matter of the brawl has been so successful that Iago now grows in confidence seeing how further manipulation might enable him to effect his full plan of revenge.

Act III, Scene i

Summary
The morning has broken and Cassio brings musicians to serenade Othello and Desdemona. The Clown is sent out to tell them to depart. Iago appears and says that he will send Emilia to Cassio

immediately, and will ensure that Othello is out of the way. Emilia is hopeful that all will be well as Desdemona is already pleading for Cassio. Even so, Cassio asks her to arrange an interview with Desdemona.

Commentary
The first two acts have been fast-moving and tense. At the beginning of this scene there is momentarily a rather heavy-handed attempt at lightening the mood with the not particularly amusing verbal quibbles of the Clown with the musicians and Cassio. This lightening of mood and releasing of tension is dramatically important in order that the tension can be built up again in the central scene of the play, III. iii, but the contrast of comic dialogue is not fully successful in the way that the Porter's comic speech just before the discovery of the king's murder is in *Macbeth*. Whereas the matter and theme of the Porter's speech is clearly related to the main action of the play, it is not easy to see that the Clown's jokes about music and flatulence are in any significant way so related. It is true that in II. i, there is music imagery and that Iago talks of untuning the harmony of the love relationship, and some tenuous connection might be made between the Clown's manipulation of words to mean something other than was intended and Iago's manipulation of situations to appear other than they are, but there is no clear pointing of these connections. Perhaps the irony of Cassio's reference to Iago as 'kind and honest' (42) and Iago's statement that he will draw Othello out of the way so that Cassio may be more free in his interview, when actually he intends to entrap him, are intended to show some connection. It is interesting to note that Desdemona appears to be interceding on Cassio's behalf even before he has asked her to do so. Again, as in the case of persuading Cassio to drink, the free actions of others rather than the manipulation of Iago seem actually to help his plan along, though here they could also have undermined it, for if Desdemona is already pleading for Cassio there is no reason why he needs to see her to ask her to do so, yet he still pursues that course of action.

Act III, Scene ii

Summary
Othello attends to his duties as governor, sending letters to the Senate, and viewing the defences of the island.

Commentary
The scene is very brief. It shows the public Othello, and suggests that he is occupied with business at the time when Cassio meets Desdemona at the opening of the next scene. Though it is very short, there is a strong dramatic irony in this scene. Just at the moment when the

security of his personal life is about to be undermined from within, Othello is inspecting the security of the island against attack from without. Like the earlier brief scene, II. ii, this one provides tragic effect through a sense of the protagonist's unawareness of what is about to happen to him.

Act III, Scene iii

Summary
Desdemona assures Cassio that she will do everything in her power to have him reinstated. When Othello enters with Iago, Cassio leaves, and Desdemona immediately begins her appeals to her husband on his behalf. When Emilia and Desdemona leave, Iago begins by remarks and insinuations to suggest that he has something on his mind related to Cassio which he is reluctant to reveal. Othello is anxious to know what it is, and Iago warns him of jealousy. Before leaving, Iago advises Othello to watch Desdemona with Cassio. Othello is troubled. When Desdemona re-enters she tries to comfort him, dropping her handkerchief as she does so. Emilia retrieves it but offers it to Iago who has often asked her to steal the handkerchief. Othello becomes more disturbed; his anger and confusion rising, he demands proof of his wife's infidelity from Iago. Iago tells him that Cassio talked in his sleep in an incriminating way and that he had seen Cassio wiping his beard with Desdemona's handkerchief. Brought to a pitch of jealous fury, Othello cries out for vengeance. Iago is to murder Cassio and Othello plans to kill Desdemona.

Commentary
This is the longest scene in the play, and its turning point. Othello begins the scene expressing his love for Desdemona but, under the influence of Iago's psychological poison, by the end he is uttering fearful threats against her life, 'I'll tear her all to pieces' (426). Commentary on the scene must focus upon the means by which Shakespeare makes such a complete change within a single scene dramatically credible. It will be important to note the way in which the scene falls into sections and how one section builds upon another. It will also be important to note the stages by which Iago works to make Othello jealous, and when particular comments or details are thrown into the conversation, for Iago's timing is impeccable as his success in this scene indicates.

The opening section in which Desdemona assures Cassio that she will not cease to plead his case with Othello shows us that by her persistence and vehemence she will certainly walk into Iago's trap. Before we see her interceding with Othello, Iago's three apparently innocent comments as Cassio leaves are the first ploys of his plot. Briefly he hints that there is something slightly suspicious going on.

He pretends that he thinks the person who has just departed could not possibly be Cassio because his sneaking away was the action of someone with a guilty conscience. Iago thus suggests a particular interpretation of what they have seen, planting a seed here which will provide a basis for later suggestions. As Desdemona and Emilia leave, Othello expresses the totality of his love for his wife –

> Perdition catch my soul
> But I do love thee! And when I love thee not
> Chaos is come again. (90–2).

The placing of this just before the process of the destruction of his love begins is dramatically powerful and provides us with a sense of the magnitude and significance of that destruction. The line, 'Chaos is come again' suggests a cosmic dimension. It was believed that the world was created by God out of chaos, a state of darkness and formlessness. The process of creation began with God's command, 'Let there be light'. For Chaos to come again suggests a reversal of the creation process, a return to darkness and disorder. What Othello is suggesting is that his world, the whole fabric of his life, would be destroyed if he no longer loved Desdemona, but Shakespeare provides the cosmic perspective in these lines linking that love to the divine force at work in creation, and to the opposition of light and darkness which is one of the primary oppositions of the play (See Section 3.1.2). Iago's activities by implication are devilish since they attempt the process of un-creation, of reversing God's works, and that process now begins.

Tentatively he asks whether Cassio knew of Othello's wooing of Desdemona. He makes no overt connection with his earlier remarks but it is implicit, and suggests that he has more on his mind than he cares to reveal. It was clear from the brawl scene (II. iii.) that one thing which stirs Othello's anger is the failure of others to be open and forthright, as when he says 'My blood begins my safer guides to rule' when he fails to get an explanation of how the brawl started first from Iago, then Cassio, and finally from Montano. Iago's ploy is always to stir up his victims (earlier Brabantio and Cassio) emotionally as a means of gaining control over them. At line 105 Othello is clearly becoming frustrated by Iago's behaviour at suggesting but not revealing something which is on his mind. He comments that there seems to be 'some monster in [his] thought/Too hideous to be shown' (106–7) as indeed there is. We recall Iago's earlier reference to his plot as a 'monstrous birth' in I. iii and Othello's reference to the brawl as monstrous (II. iii, 221). The image here is of a dangerous creature which is about to be let out of Iago's mind — 'As if thou then hadst shut up in thy brain/Some horrible conceit' (113–14).

Before going any further, Iago makes sure of Othello's trust and belief in his loyalty and honesty, 'My lord, you know I love you'

(115). The statement, almost a question, receives a confirmation of Othello's trust, and an indication that he is already disturbed by Iago's hesitation – 'these stops of thine affright me'. Having confirmed Othello's trust in him, Iago then moves on to talk of Cassio's honesty whilst subtly suggesting that perhaps it should be doubted. He does not say 'I dare be sworn that he is honest', but 'I dare be sworn I think that he is honest', and though he makes a general statement 'Men should be what they seem', the 'should be' seems to imply that perhaps Cassio of whom he has been speaking may not be. The irony of these words about outward appearance coming from Iago is evident.

Having confirmed Othello's trust in him and hinted at Cassio's dishonesty whilst ostensibly protesting his honesty, Iago is more sure of his ground and proceeds to suggest that he does indeed have suspicions about Cassio but blames himself for having what are probably just evil thoughts. He says that it would not be right to utter them and that Othello should take no notice. Ironically, Iago speaks of the importance of reputation, having scoffed at it to Cassio in II. iii, saying that he would not wish to express unfounded suspicions of Cassio which might destroy his reputation as an honest man. Iago has moved from mere hints to confirmation that there is indeed something on his mind, and Othello becomes more desperate to know what it is. Whilst pretending to maintain his integrity by not telling Othello, Iago now releases the 'monster'. He has said nothing which would indicate that Othello should have reason to be jealous, but now by warning him of jealousy he suggests that there may be something about which to be jealous,

> Oh beware, my lord, of jealousy!
> It is the green-eyed monster, which doth mock
> The meat it feeds on. (163–5)

Othello's assurance that he would not be jealous simply on hearsay but would need to have proof allows Iago to move on further to suggest that he should observe Desdemona and Cassio. We notice that Othello suggests that unfounded jealousy makes a man irrational like an animal:

> Exchange me for a goat
> When I shall turn the business of my soul
> To such exsufflicate and blown surmises. (178–80)

Having established in Othello's mind that there might be reasons for doubting Cassio, Iago now moves to the more difficult task of persuading the Moor that Desdemona is deceiving him. He begins by saying that he knows what Venetian women are like. He thus reminds

Othello that he is not himself a Venetian, and that he, Iago, has a better knowledge of such matters. Othello's question, 'Dost thou say so?' suggests that the ploy has worked. He begins to feel on uncertain ground, to be aware that perhaps he is not equipped by experience to assess the truth of what he is being told. This indication of vulnerability is followed by a telling thrust from Iago, the reminder of Brabantio's warning (I. iii.) that Desdemona has deceived her father and may deceive her husband. Iago is on much more dangerous ground here in implying suspicion of Desdemona, and before proceeding further he covers himself by assuring Othello that he is only saying these things out of love and concern for his master:

> But I am much to blame.
> I humbly do beseech you of your pardon
> For too much loving you. (209–11)

Othello's response indicates that Iago is on safe ground to proceed; 'I am bound to you forever' both indicates that he believes the ensign and implies the result of that belief.

Iago tests the effects of what he has said by remarking that Othello's spirits seem to have been dashed. Othello's denial is perhaps the first indication in the play of a response that is not totally honest and open, as he tries to cover up his feelings. Doubts begin to emerge; assertion of Desdemona's honesty is juxtaposed to 'And yet, how nature erring from itself' (225). Before he can finish this statement which again reveals a weakness, Iago moves in to bolster the doubt – 'Ay, there's the point' – and to do so in terms which he could not possibly have safely used earlier. He draws attention to Desdemona's rejection of many Venetian suitors, people of her own race and colour, and he suggests that her marriage to Othello was unnatural, indicating 'a will most rank'; in other words he implies the lascivious inclinations that he suggested in his attempts to persuade Roderigo that Desdemona might still be his. The fact that Iago can go so far and not receive a violent and angry response from Othello is indicative of how sure of his ground he now is and how far he has succeeded in unsettling the Moor's faith in his wife. His ploys of hinting, implication, and denials which actually seem to confirm, have the effect of suggesting there is much more to be revealed. Apart from his assertions of love for Othello and Cassio, Iago has not stated anything that is untrue; it is the way he has expressed himself and his insinuations that are insidious. Even his apparent attempts to calm or console, particularly in his delayed exit, when he returns to beg Othello not to give too much credence to what he has said, have the effect of conveying an impression that he is trying to shield Othello from some terrible truth.

For the first time in the play Othello is given a soliloquy, and this in itself indicates the effect of Iago's plot on him at this point. So far the soliloquy has been a form of utterance associated with Iago, appropriately so because this convention reveals inner thoughts which are hidden in the interactions with other characters. Shakespeare has not needed to give Othello a soliloquy until this moment because his words and actions have openly revealed his inner being and thoughts. Now he speaks, in a mode associated with Iago, things which he would not yet say directly to others. This indication of the way in which Iago's poison is working on him is reinforced by the imagery; he uses an image which is totally uncharacteristic of the noble and heroic Moor we have seen until now – 'I had rather be a toad/And live upon the vapour of a dungeon' (267–8). Unpleasant animal images are characteristic of Iago rather than of Othello and this image is indicative of how he has affected Othello's mind. The toad was believed by the Elizabethans to be poisonous and it was one of the creatures associated with witches. Thus the image is connected with image series of animals, poison, and witchcraft, which are associated thoughout the play. The lines present Othello changed to an animal, and to a poisonous and evil creature at that, which is exactly the transformation Iago wishes to effect.

However, the ensign has not yet been completely successful. There is still the chance that Othello may not succumb totally as Desdemona appears and her appearance reassures Othello of her virtue. Her gentle action in trying to soothe his headache leads to the dropping of the fatal handkerchief, an event which Iago had not engineered but which he quickly sees he can use for the furtherance of his designs. As Othello returns, Iago underlines the changes that have occurred. His poison is now working on Othello, who will never again enjoy peace of mind. It is clear that Othello, presumably as a result of being with Desdemona whose gentleness and love must have confused him further about what he should believe, is now in an overwrought state. He speaks with some violence and passion, and turns on Iago – 'Avaunt! Be gone! Thou hast set me on the rack' (331). He speaks as if he now believes his wife's infidelity to be a fact (334), and sees the world collapsing around him, chaos coming again. The famous 'Farewell' speech shows Othello bidding adieu to the very things which define him as a person. This is a farewell to himself, to the person we have known up to this point. Now a transformed Othello turns on the 'honest' Iago calling him a villain, and threatening him with a ferocity which must have even the cunning and resourceful ensign worried about the forces he has unleashed. After all, Othello might be so carried away by passion and anger that he might kill Iago too. Iago cunningly laments that this is the treatment he receives for being honest, and, ironically, at this moment when he is intent on transforming Othello from the noble man to a beast, he appeals to his humanity, 'Are you a man?' (370), indicating that

Othello is behaving in an irrational and furious manner unbefitting a
human being. This calms Othello a little in his approach to Iago, but
he shows he is in a state of confusion and simply does not know what
to believe – I think my wife be honest, and think she is not;/I think
that thou art just, and think thou art not' (380–1). Now Iago offers to
provide a means of ending his uncertainty and of ascertaining the
truth. He asks Othello what he would regard as proof, saying
shrewdly that it would be difficult to catch Desdemona and Cassio in
the act, but then giving an account of Cassio talking in his sleep,
which, though no proof at all, is accepted as such by Othello in his
already overwrought state, and calls forth from him the terrible
savage cry, 'I'll tear her all to pieces' (426). This is a Moor who is
reverting to the barbarous state of 'the Cannibals that each other
eat,/The Anthropophagi' (I. iii, 142–3) under Iago's influence. Earlier it was Othello who had demanded clear proof, but now it is the
ensign who in a further subtle ploy insists that Cassio's words were
only spoken in a dream and cannot be held to prove anything, though
they may heighten suspicion. At this point, having only recently
gained possession of it, he uses the handkerchief to provide more
tangible evidence, saying that he has seen it in Cassio's possession.
Now Othello totally succumbs to Iago's wiles. His love has changed
to hate; he blows it to heaven, summoning from hell the spirit of
'black vengeance'. Iago has made Othello like himself, a man
consumed by hatred who desires revenge. The 'Like to the Pontic
sea' speech by its grandiloquence – use of proper nouns referring to
distant places, epic simile, energy and rhythmic sweep – shows that
Othello is not completely changed, but the speech indicates through
its imagery that his noble and heroic energies are now irreversibly
directed towards destruction; through the image he associates himself
with the sea and elemental forces, which elsewhere in the play are
presented as threatening destruction, as in the storm scene. Othello
kneels as he vows his intention to pursue vengeance and Iago kneels
beside him, devoting himself 'To wronged Othello's service'. His
final line in the scene, 'I am yours forever', makes us think of the
marriage vows and see how the relationship between Othello and
Iago has supplanted that between Othello and Desdemona.

Act III, Scene iv

Summary
Desdemona shows concern about the loss of her handkerchief.
Othello arrives and attempts to hide his disturbed emotional state.
Desdemona begins to plead for Cassio. Othello asks her for the
handkerchief, telling her it had magical properties. Under pressure
Desdemona insists that it is not lost and tries to divert attention to the
reinstatement of Cassio, but this only enrages Othello who leaves in

anger. Desdemona assures Cassio that she will do her utmost for him and she decides to go to find Othello. Bianca, a prostitute who has fallen in love with Cassio, appears and accuses him of staying away from her. He gives her the handkerchief which he has found in his lodgings asking her to copy the design of it, but Bianca immediately assumes it must be a love token from a new mistress, and is jealous. Promising to visit her soon, Cassio sees Bianca on her way.

Commentary
After a long scene of increasing tension, Shakespeare again introduces the Clown to provide a brief moment in which the mood is lightened before building up the tension again later in the scene. Dramatically it would not be possible to sustain the intensity of the previous scene, particularly in its latter part, and the audience would not be able to bear such emotionally-charged situations without some break or release. The humour is of a rather undistinguished kind, linked with the main action by the way in which the Clown interprets the meaning of Desdemona's words incorrectly. This might be seen to reflect the misinterpretation of her words and actions by Othello, though the parallel is not strongly pointed.

The brief exchange between Desdemona and Emilia which follows provides yet another moment of dramatic irony in which the audience sees characters in a state of supposed security just before disaster is about to occur. Desdemona, worried about the loss of the handkerchief, comforts herself with the thought that Othello is not a jealous man and will not misinterpret its loss.

When Othello enters Shakespeare gives him a significant aside which indicates how Iago's poison is destroying him – 'Oh hardness to dissemble!'. The aside, like the soliloquy, is a dramatic convention of the time that gives the audience access to a character's real thoughts which may not be indicated by his words and actions towards other characters. It has been Iago who has been given asides until now because he is a character whose outward appearance belies his inner nature and intentions. That Othello now has an aside and one which makes clear that he is dissembling, shows how the integrity of the noble Moor in which outward appearance and inner nature corresponded, is being destroyed, and he is being torn apart. He must pretend that he does not know of Desdemona's 'infidelity'.

It is not clear whether Othello's speeches about the handkerchief and its origins (55–75) are part of his play-acting or are intended to indicate what he really believes. The fact that it is not made clear that he is dissembling here tends to invest the handkerchief with mystery and significance. Othello makes it a symbol of wedded love, the loss of which 'were such perdition/As nothing else could match' (67–68). We may also see these speeches as indicative of the Christian Othello reverting to superstition and belief in witchcraft, thus presenting another aspect of the metamorphosis which Iago is effecting in him, a relinquishing of Christian and civilised values for primitive and instinctive life-responses.

The destructiveness of Iago's poison also has an effect on Desdemona. Under the pressure of Othello's questioning she lies about the handkerchief, saying that it is not lost. When she tries to deflect the subject back to Cassio's reinstatement, she only increases Othello's emotional disturbance and he leaves as the situation becomes intolerable for him. Now, in relation to their earlier conversation, Emilia asks Desdemona whether she can still say Othello is not a jealous man. Desdemona tries to account for his actions by putting the blame on the worries of his public duties, but the conversation reverts to jealousy, which here again is described as a monster (157–9) and one which is preying on Othello's mind. We recall the caged monster of Iago's thought from the previous scene, which he has released.

The final section of the scene between Cassio and Bianca provides us with another example of unfounded jealousy, this time that of a woman, but also provoked by the handkerchief.

Act IV, Scene i

Summary

Iago works on Othello's imagination, conjuring up pictures of his wife in bed with a lover. He lays added stress on the handkerchief as proof. Iago hesitatingly reports what Cassio has said. Othello collapses in a fit. When he regains consciousness, Iago tells him how he shall have proof by secretly watching Cassio's expression when Iago questions him about Desdemona. When the former lieutenant arrives, instead of talking about Desdemona, Iago speaks about Bianca, provoking Cassio to laughter and mockery. Othello, observing but unable to hear, believes this is directed at his wife. Quite by chance Bianca arrives with the handkerchief. Othello recognises it as Desdemona's and is convinced of his wife's guilt. He plans to strangle her whilst Iago will kill Cassio. Lodovico arrives from Venice with official papers recalling Othello and appointing Cassio as governor in his place. When Desdemona says she is glad of the news Othello strikes her in public and then humiliates her by calling her back at Lodovico's request. Lodovico marvels at the change in the noble Moor.

Commentary

Compared with III. iii, Iago's assault upon Othello's credulity and imagination is much less subtle. He is now sure of his ground, certain that Othello has already been so emotionally disturbed that he will accept as truths things he would not have accepted earlier. Iago is thus able to take greater risks and to be more explicit in his suggestions. He forces Othello to imagine his wife in bed with Cassio as a means of bringing him to a new intensity of jealousy, just as in his treatment of Brabantio and Cassio earlier he had made them imagine Desdemona having sexual intercourse with Othello as a means of making them lose their control. Shakespeare provides a powerful theatrical image of the destruction of Othello as he physically collapses under the pressure of the mental pictures summoned up by Iago. At this moment of collapse he speaks not in the majestic blank verse by which he has been defined as a character earlier in the play, but in prose, and in prose that is disjointed and becoming inarticulate, suggesting powerful feelings but often lacking the syntactical structure which would give the utterance coherent meaning. Linguistically chaos has come, and he ends by calling Desdemona 'devil'. Iago's attempt to turn her virtue into pitch has totally succeeded, and in doing so he has completely transformed the noble Othello. It is significant that this moment depends upon a word, 'lie', which has a double meaning, suggesting either falsehood or sexual intercourse. Iago's use of the word (33) in a sentence which is unfinished could have had either meaning, but Othello immediately seizes upon the second. Yet the suggestion that Cassio lay with Desdemona is, as we know, a falsehood. Thus both meanings of the word are present and we are made aware linguistically of a situation which depends upon mistaken interpretations and meanings.

As Othello returns to consciousness the dialogue emphasises contrasts between men and animals. Othello, believing himself to be a cuckold, says that such a man is 'a monster and a beast'; Iago's intention is to reduce him to a bestial state and ironically he counsels Othello four times to bear his ills with courage and fortitude 'like a man' (62, 66, 78, 90).

The power of deceptive appearance is emphasised as Othello watches Iago and Cassio in conversation about Desdemona, as he thinks, but actually about Bianca. We note the stark contrast between Cassio's respectful attitude towards Desdemona in earlier scenes and his flippant, mocking attitude when speaking of Bianca. At an opportune moment chance plays into Iago's hands with Bianca's appearance carrying the handkerchief. It is noticeable that, though Iago is a cunning plotter, at a number of points circumstances over which he has no control contribute to the success of his plots. Bianca's jealousy over the handkerchief contributes to the focus of this scene on the power of false appearance to cause disruption in human relationships, which the next section of the scene emphasises as Othello plans to murder Cassio and Desdemona, uttering the dreadful cry, 'I will chop her into messes' (210), a line which powerfully suggests his descent into savagery, and again links him with the Cannibals, the Anthropophagi. His transformation is further emphasised as he calls for poison, which has been associated earlier in the play with Iago, to kill Desdemona.

The central part of the play has concentrated upon Othello's personal life. The next section reminds us of the world of public affairs which until his marriage had been Othello's natural sphere. His recall to Venice and particularly his replacement as governor by Cassio comes as a further blow. Not only has Cassio, he believes, supplanted him in his wife's affections, he has now supplanted him in public office. The control which we noted in earlier public scenes is not strong enough to suppress the anger and hurt which he feels. When the news pleases Desdemona, Othello assumes she is pleased for her supposed lover's advancement, whereas she is probably pleased that they will be returning to Venice, associated with her first love for Othello, and leaving Cyprus where her marriage night had been disturbed by a brawl and unknown circumstances seem to be changing and disturbing her husband. The degradation of the noble Othello is taken a stage further as he now calls his wife 'Devil!' in public, strikes her, and creates public embarrassment by calling her back at Lodovico's request. We see that the emotional pressure is such that again Othello's speeches reveal linguistic breakdown. The speech beginning at line 261 begins with the repetition of 'turn', 'weep' and 'obedient', and then becomes disjointed as Othello speaks first to Lodovico, then to Desdemona, turning several times from one to the other. Finally, he leaves crying 'Goats and monkeys', seemingly incoherent in the public setting, but expressing an overwhelming condemnation of lechery, as these animals were believed to be particularly sexually active. Lodovico's bewildered lament, 'Is this the noble Moor. . .', reminds us of the Othello of the earlier public scenes and stresses the transformation which has taken place. Shakespeare places this speech here so that we should not forget the former Othello, and we should be aware of how great a change has occurred.

Act IV, Scene ii

Summary
Othello questions Emilia about his wife and Cassio. At his command she brings Desdemona to him, and a painful exchange ensues in which she protests her innocence but can say nothing to convince her husband, who finally leaves, calling her a whore. Desdemona tries to understand Othello's behaviour. Iago's assistance is sought, and she asks him what she should do to placate Othello. He makes a show of attempting to reassure her. The scene ends with Iago drawing Roderigo into a plot to kill Cassio.

Commentary

Othello is apparently seeking evidence from Emilia, but it is clear that he now wants confirmation of Desdemona's guilt, and will not listen to any report which might deny it. His jealousy and irrationality have gone so far that he will not trust what is said to him. He dismisses Emilia's assertion that Desdemona is a pure and exemplary wife by saying that any bawd could make such a statement about a prostitute. Having been made aware of the possibility of deceptive appearance, and changed from the man who thought everyone honest because he himself was so, he seems to believe that all appearances must be false, and that Desdemona's apparent purity and piety are actually indications of how cunning she is in disguising her lascivious nature. Desdemona's protestations of innocence are ignored. There is nothing that she can say which will convince him that she is true to him, and when she swears she is Othello's 'true and loyal wife', he tells her she is damning herself by telling a lie. The full extent of Iago's success is indicated by the concern here with the word 'honest': Othello totally disbelieves in Desdemona's honesty and believes in Iago's. In his mind the fair has become foul, and the recurrence of the image of toads in a dark place in Othello's speech (60–1) which we first noted at III. iii, 267–8, indicates Iago's penetration of his mind. In the earlier scene Othello applied the image to himself, but here it is applied in an obscene way to Desdemona's supposed lovers. She was 'a fountain' providing the source of his life and being, an image suggesting running water and upward movement, associated with purity and health. Now he thinks of her as a cistern, well, or hole, an image suggesting depths, darkness and still, or stagnant, water in which toads copulate and spawn. This detail shows just how infected he is by Iago's poison, as the obscenity and nastiness of the image reflect the prurience and coarseness of the ensign's own references to sexual intercourse at various points in the play. Heaven and hell contrasts are also strong in this scene, as Desdemona, whom he has publicly called 'devil', is associated in his mind with all that is evil. She is as 'false as hell' (38); the expression of Patience like 'young and rose-lipped cherubin' (62) turns 'grim as hell'; 'Heaven stops the nose' at the offence Desdemona is supposed to have committed (76); and finally Emilia is presented as the keeper of the gates of hell (89–91). The chief contrast of all in this scene is between the innocent which Desdemona actually is, and the whore which Othello believes her to be and repeatedly calls her.

The belief that his wife is a whore has the corollary of making him believe himself to be a cuckold, traditionally, and frequently in the comedies of the period, a figure of ridicule –

> But alas, to make me
> The fixed figure for the time of scorn
> To point his slow and moving finger at (52–4) –

a figure very different from the valiant Moor respected and honoured by the Venetian Senate. Though Othello goes on to say that he could have borne this humiliation and that the more intolerable fact is that the source of his being has been polluted, the fact that he mentions it shows that it has had its effect on him. We may see in this speech a strong element of self-concern, which is again indicative of the spirit of Iago.

When Othello leaves, Desdemona is in a state of shock. At first Emilia can get little response from her and her words suggest that she feels she has lost Othello. At this point, ironically, she turns for help to the very instigator of the plot against her, calling him 'good friend' (148). Ironically, too, Emilia lights upon the truth in trying to find an explanation for Othello's behaviour; someone has slandered Desdemona in order to get some office. Significantly she reminds Iago of the way in which he was made jealous by a story that she, Emilia, had been unfaithful with Othello. Shakespeare reminds us at this point of this detail from Iago's second soliloquy, because it underlines the way in which Iago's plot springs from envy of others' 'quiet' or happiness, and a desire to reduce them to the same state as himself.

In her anguish Desdemona nevertheless affirms the strength and endurance of her love:

> Unkindness may do much,
> And his unkindness may defeat my life,
> But never taint my love. (157–9)

The total selflessness of her words contrasts strongly with Othello's self-concern earlier in the scene and serves to underline that it is he, not she, whose integrity has been destroyed. Desdemona's love has been assaulted in the most terrible way by Othello, she has been profoundly disturbed, and is clearly in an emotionally-overwrought state, but her love remains unalterable. As Desdemona makes this affirmation of her love in Iago's presence, she kneels, a gesture which may remind us of the vows of Othello and Iago as they kneel at the end of III. iii, thus establishing a contrast between hate and love.

As Iago's plot seems to be succeeding, Roderigo presents a threat which might upset it. Exasperated with endlessly providing money and jewels to try to persuade Desdemona to look favourably at him, he intends to speak directly to her. His weakness is revealed as he is again manipulated by Iago who tells him that he is on the brink of success, and persuades him to agree to a plot to kill Cassio.

Act IV, Scene iii

Summary
Othello sends Desdemona to bed, telling her to dismiss Emilia. Alone with her mistress, Emilia tells her that she has put the wedding

sheets on her bed as she requested. Desdemona asks that if she dies before Emilia, she should wrap her corpse in one of the sheets. In melancholy mood she sings a song which she first heard from her mother's maid who had a similar experience of unhappy love. Near tears she talks with Emilia about fidelity in marriage.

Commentary
This scene is full of foreboding. The detail of the wedding sheets being put on the bed and the mention of Desdemona's death link marriage and death in a way that will be particularly significant in the final scene. The foreboding is increased as Desdemona cannot get out of her mind the willow song of her mother's maid, Barbary, another example of forsaken love, who sang the song when she died. The song creates a mood of pathos, which emphasises Desdemona's vulnerability. The stillness and the gentle sadness of this scene contrast with the emotional anguish and violence of the previous one and the physical violence of the scene which follows.

The absoluteness of Desdemona's love and of her spiritual worth is emphasised by the contrast which is established between her and Emilia in their attitudes towards fidelity in marriage. Innocently, Desdemona asks if there really are women who 'abuse their husbands/In such gross kind?' (59–60). She affirms 'by this heavenly light' that she would never do such a thing for the whole world. Emilia, attempting perhaps to try to relieve Desdemona's melancholy, by picking up her words twists them so that they have another meaning. The phrase, 'by this heavenly light', which Desdemona uses in the form of a vow emphasising spiritual and moral values which govern her behaviour, becomes in Emilia's mouth literally the sun, or daylight as opposed to darkness. She would not be unfaithful in view of the world but she might be if it were hidden. Whilst this works on a human level as an attempt, albeit perhaps rather clumsy and insensitive on Emilia's part, to prevent the anguish of the situation overwhelming them both, it also works in dramatic terms by drawing contrasts between the spiritual and worldly perspectives of Desdemona and Emilia respectively, presenting unshakeable goodness and worth in the former and emphasising how deceived Othello is, immediately before the last act of the tragedy.

Emilia blames husbands for the infidelities of their wives, which she presents as revenge for ill-treatment and infidelity on the husbands' parts. The mention of revenge, and from Emilia's mouth, should remind us perhaps of Iago from whose desire for revenge the whole tragic action has stemmed. From a mistaken sense of broken trust, in Emilia and in Othello, has sprung a chain of consequences which are proving fatal. Desdemona's final lines in this scene present a different and essentially creative approach to suffering, not to produce more suffering but to learn from it. Thus the act ends with the Iago values and the Desdemona values clearly juxtaposed, and the central conflict of the play is stated.

Act V, Scene i

Summary
Cassio makes his way from Bianca's house and is set upon in the darkness by Roderigo. He wounds his assailant, and Iago, unseen, wounds Cassio in the leg and runs off. Othello on his way to Desdemona hears cries and conflict in the darkness, and is spurred on to kill Desdemona by Iago's example in dealing with Cassio. Lodovico and Gratiano arrive and try in the darkness to discover what has happened. Iago then enters with a light. Cassio tells him that one of his attackers is lying wounded somewhere nearby. Iago kills Roderigo and then attends to Cassio's wounds. At that moment Bianca enters and Iago immediately accuses her of complicity in a plot to kill Cassio. She is arrested and led away.

Commentary
This scene takes place in darkness, and a darkness thicker than that of any previous night scene. Repeatedly words and actions indicate the characters' inability to see each other and to know exactly what is happening. Only Iago moves through the darkness knowing all and in control. All this serves to emphasise that the play has reached its final stage. The darkness of the mind which Iago has created has extinguished the light of understanding and faith, and truth has been lost. The consequences will be disastrous. This is a scene of confused activity in which Iago is able to wound Cassio without being seen and to kill Roderigo while others are present. The arrivals of Lodovico and Gratiano, then Bianca, and finally Emilia, maintain an impression of urgency and activity, as do the brief appearance of Othello and the comings and goings of Iago.

Moving about in the darkness, bringing mutilation and death, Iago is most obviously devil-like, but the scene emphasises his human vulnerability. His plotting has been so detailed and subtle that there is a danger that the deceptions he has woven may be exposed. Roderigo presents a threat as he wants the jewels and money back, and by talking to Cassio about what Iago has told him, Othello may discover the deception that has been practised. It is in Iago's interests that both Cassio and Roderigo die. As he says in the last lines of the scene, the events of this night will either make him or destroy him. We should not be so confident of Iago's successful villainy as to miss the tension for him inherent in the present situation. Though he stresses the need to be rid of Cassio for fear of exposure, he also suggests another familiar motive: 'He hath a daily beauty in his life/That makes me ugly' (19–20). We see here yet again the desire to destroy qualities in others which he does not possess himself, or which make him painfully aware of his own deficiencies. The accusation and arrest of the innocent Bianca at the end of the scene helps to cover his own tracks but at the same time it is a blow aimed at love, motivated perhaps by a desire to destroy Bianca because she loved Cassio.

The irony of Iago's deceptive appearance is evident throughout the scene. Othello calls him 'brave Iago, honest and just' (31) just after he has severely wounded Cassio under cover of darkness; Lodovico calls him 'a very valiant fellow' (52); and it is Iago who carries the only light in the scene. In his double-dealing role, Iago ironically accuses himself as he exclaims against Cassio's attackers 'Oh treacherous villains.' (58). He hypocritically calls Cassio 'brother' and 'my dear friend', and shows himself apparently concerned in every way to help him, binding his wound with his own shirt and calling for Othello's surgeon. When Bianca comes he accuses her of setting Roderigo on to kill Cassio, saying that she has a guilty appearance, and that even if nothing is said guilt is always evident. This is the height of irony from the man who is guilty of all that has happened in the scene, and it emphasises how plausible he is to everyone as a good and honest man.

Act V, Scene ii

Summary
Though he feels a sense of conflict between the deed he must perform to punish infidelity and his attraction to Desdemona's beauty, Othello eventually smothers her. Emilia arrives with the news of the death of Roderigo and the wounding of Cassio. She discovers Desdemona dying. Othello tells her that Iago had revealed Desdemona's adultery. When Emilia rails against Othello he threatens her and she calls for help. Montano, Gratiano and Iago arrive. Emilia reveals how she had given the handkerchief to Iago, and Othello, for the first time, perceives the villainy of Iago, who stabs Emilia and runs out. Cassio is brought in and tells Othello how he came by the handkerchief. With the completeness of the deception that has been practised upon him revealed, Othello kills himself.

Commentary
This is another night scene. The fact that in the previous scene Iago had been the only person with light helps to suggest a connection with him as Othello enters the darkened bedroom carrying a torch. The irony of Iago bearing a light in a scene of confusion and deception which he himself has engineered is evident. There is irony too in Othello as light-bearer when he has been so totally overcome by falsehood and the evil machinations of Iago. Visually the light–dark contrasts of the play are emphasised at the opening of the scene.

When Othello enters he is not in the murderous mood of the Act IV scenes – he does not come in prepared to 'chop her into messes' – nor even in the threatening and vindictive mood of his rather melodramatic lines from the previous scene:

> Strumpet, I come!
> Forth of my heart those charms, thine eyes, are blotted.
> Thy bed, lust-stained, shall with lust's blood be spotted.
>
> (V. i, 34–6)

Now he says 'I'll not shed her blood,/Nor scar that whiter skin of hers than snow' (3–4). What Shakespeare presents here is the complexity of Othello's feelings, and the conflict between what he thinks is a rational and moral public duty and the tender but strong sensuous attraction which he still feels towards Desdemona. The opening lines suggest by repetition that he is only able to bring himself to kill his wife by repeating to himself that in so doing he is acting not from personal motives of jealousy and anger but as an agent of moral justice – 'It is the cause . . . she must die, else she'll betray more men.' He presents his act not as a murder but as a sacrifice (67). It is not simply the sacrifice of Desdemona for impurity but a sacrifice on his own part of his beloved in the interests of morality and public good. As he weeps over the woman for whom he still feels such tenderness and attraction, he says 'This sorrow's heavenly –/It strikes where it doth love' (21–2). The implication here is that as God sacrificed his beloved son for the good of mankind, so Othello will sacrifice his love for that good. We recall that Othello had told the Senate that he would not allow his personal life to interfere with his public duties if Desdemona were to accompany him to Cyprus, and the brawl scene of Act II showed his personal life disturbed by public events which he dealt with in a responsible manner, subordinating personal pleasure and his friendship for Cassio to what he saw as the public order requirements of the situation. Othello's sense of personal integrity derives in part from his public service. When we first see him in I. ii, he says of Brabantio's case, 'My services, which I have done the Signory/Shall out-tongue his complaints' (I. ii, 18–19), and his final speech begins, 'Soft you, a word or two before you go./I have done the state some service, and they know't' (337–8).

As the scene opens, therefore, we see Othello trying to assume a public role, to distance himself from the deed, presenting it as an act of justice. It is not his sword but the sword of Justice which will kill Desdemona (17). This perhaps indicates the psychological need for him to restore that sense of personal worth and integrity which his wife's supposed infidelity had destroyed. The speech however, is full of conflict, between the public role he tries to force himself to assume and his personal response to Desdemona. Her skin is whiter than snow, 'smooth as monumental alabaster'; she is a rose giving off perfume, and her breath is 'balmy' as he kisses her. The response is intensely sensuous, a response to the physical presence of Desdemona, but it also convinces by its tenderness that Othello has not lost his love for his wife. Indeed, he says, 'Be thus when thou art dead, and I will kill thee/And love thee after' (18–19). It is this which makes the scene so poignant and so painful to watch, rather than simply violent and sensational as it would have been had Othello completely lost his love for Desdemona and had entered with a single-minded purpose to destroy her. The intensity of the speech is increased by Othello's sense of the finality of the deed. The image of light is connected with life. Othello says that if he puts out the flaming torch he carries, it is possible to relight it, but he will not be able to bring Desdemona back to life if he kills her. The image of the rose is also used, an image traditionally associated with beauty; once plucked the rose cannot be put back on the tree to live again. We notice a hint of uncertainty as Othello says that if he puts out the torch, 'I can again thy former light restore./Should I repent me', which indicates that he does not approach this deed single-mindedly and with absolute conviction. There is, he admits to himself, a possibility that he will regret the deed when it is done. This highlights the conflict in the speech and that it is with great difficulty that Othello assumes the role of agent of Justice.

Othello's sense of the deed as a sacrifice, an action in support of morality and religion, is further evidenced by his concern that before she dies Desdemona should have the opportunity to confess all her sins so that she may die in a state of repentance. Although in previous scenes we noted signs of how Iago's poison brought to the surface primitive emotions and caused a reversion to savagery in Othello's responses, there is nothing of that here. He will sacrifice Desdemona for the cause of morality and justice, but he is concerned about the state of her Christian soul. In this we see a concern too that the deed should be not an act of personal vengeance committed in a state of passion, but a ritual act, committed in a careful and calm manner according to the rules. However, Desdemona's comments about his rolling eyes and his gnawing his nether lip further indicate the conflict between the public role he wishes to assume and his personal feelings. She says 'Some bloody passion shakes your very frame.'

Desdemona's denials of her guilt, if true, would make Othello's action, as he sees it, 'A murder, which I thought a sacrifice' (68). This disturbs him so that he becomes more passionate in his accusations, calling Desdemona 'strumpet' and refusing now her request to say one prayer. The periodic sentences and poetic force of the opening speech give way to terse dialogue, sometimes single words or half-lines only given to Othello. When he has killed Desdemona, we are given a longer speech (94–104) but it is disjointed with brief sentences and phrases, expressive of a state of shock and of the uncertainty and sense of disintegration which the murder produces. It is only at the end of the speech that the longer sentences and natural or cosmic imagery associated with the noble Moor emerge, and then it is an image of darkness:

> Methinks it should be now a huge eclipse
> Of sun and moon, and that th'affrighted globe
> Should yawn at alteration. (102–4).

Yet the emptiness of this image is apparent. The words 'it should be now' draw our attention to the fact that there is no disturbance in the heavens accompanying this act, but there is simply Othello with his murdered wife on the bed, not knowing what to do as Emilia hammers on the door. The contrast between the heroic – how things should be – and the reality – how things are – is striking, and this emphasises both how hollow and self-deceptive was the attempt to take on the role of agent of Justice, and also how far from the Othello of the opening is the man who now asks 'What is best to do?' and who is concerned that Emilia will discover Desdemona's body. It is here if anywhere that we are shown Othello destroyed. In the scenes of jealous fury he was transformed by Iago's poison, but just as his virtues and nobility raised him above others, so his passionate and ferocious anger was on a grand scale as in the 'Like to the Pontic sea' speech (III. iii, 448ff.). That speech also showed him decisive and determined as he was in the earlier scenes in Acts I and II. Now, momentarily at least, he is reduced to indecision and a concern to hide what he has done from Emilia. The image of eclipse contains not only the idea of cataclysm (eclipses were believed to portend terrible events), and the idea of darkness (blackness) connected with mourning, but also of darkness providing a cover to hide the truth. We are here far from the openness of the Othello of Act I. This impression is strengthened by his reactions to the news that Cassio is still alive, 'Not Cassio killed! Then murder's out of tune/And sweet revenge grows harsh', and his threatening of Emilia with his sword. Set against this are the utterly selfless and loving final words of Desdemona who tells Emilia that she has killed herself, and then says, 'Commend me to my lord.' Momentarily Othello is prepared to hide behind Desdemona's words (129) and then he seems to see her selfless attempt to shield him only as another proof of how given to lying she was. He then has to justify himself by telling Emilia of the believed adultery with Cassio. In doing so, he reveals Iago's part in the events, and Emilia is taken aback. Four times she exclaims, 'My husband!' unable to believe what she has heard, and Othello, characteristically exasperated by this repetition, emphatically says,

> He, woman;
> I say thy husband; dost understand the word?
> My friend, thy husband, honest, honest Iago. (152–4)

The repetition of the word 'honest' at this moment emphasises the completeness of Othello's trust in Iago which is just about to be destroyed as Emilia confronts her husband.

As Othello sees clearly for the first time since the middle of Act III, the personal qualities he had lost in the period of his confusion begin to re-emerge. He sees the falsehood of Iago, and, by doing so, the honesty of Desdemona. He momentarily tries a return to heroic swashbuckling action as, disarmed, he takes another sword from a hiding place – 'I have another weapon in this chamber;/It was a sword of Spain, the ice-brook's temper' (252–3) – and goes on to recall his military exploits with this weapon as he contemplates fighting his way out of the room. This is an important speech because it recalls for us the Othello of the past, and it shows, through Othello's own recognition of the fact, that this kind of apparently brave and heroic action is now empty of meaning. He would be fighting to survive to live a life which has lost its significance by Desdemona's death. Heroic action in the past had sprung from integrity and nobility. To fight his way out of the room would merely be the action of a murderer trying to escape. In imagery of a sea journey, he acknowledges that his life ends with Desdemona's. As he asks 'Where should Othello go?', his movement towards the bed shows that he knows the answer. The images of Othello tormented in hell show how his understanding has progressed. From the idea of fighting his way out, possibly killing others in the process, into a meaningless future, he moves to a view of himself as a slave, and he appeals to the devils to punish him for his crimes. As agent there can no longer be any meaning for him, but as passive sufferer there is. His reply to Lodovico's question, 'Where is this rash and most unfortunate man?' indicates his own sense of the loss of his former identity – 'That's he that was Othello: here I am.'

Cassio's entry provides the opportunity for Othello to ask his pardon, and for the unfolding of the final details which remain for him to learn, leading to the acknowledgement of himself, thrice, as fool (322).

Othello's final speech, a source of much critical controversy and conflicting interpretations (see Chapter 3) provides, in my view, the logical conclusion to the development which has been traced in this scene. The language and style remind us of the noble Othello of the first part of the play, and indeed there is in these last moments some renewal of his greatness of spirit, or restoration of integrity, which comes from an acknowledgement of what he has become – like the base Indian and the malignant Turk – and from appropriate action upon that knowledge. Iago had transformed him into a 'Turk', with all the connotations that term carries in the play; the old Othello was the fighter for truth and civilisation against the falsity and barbarousness of the Turks, and the only way the old Othello can reassert itself is by killing the Turk that he himself has become. Thus he re-enacts in his last moment an incident from earlier times, and in doing so he is both the noble Othello and the Turk. It is an image of killing the evil part of himself and thus restoring his integrity. He dies affirming his love for Desdemona in a final kiss.

3 THEMES AND ISSUES

3.1 OPPOSITIONS

It is easily assumed that the major themes of Othello are jealousy and appearance and reality, but we shall reach only a superficial understanding if we go no further than this. The play presents a situation in which the central character becomes jealous, but it is not fundamentally about jealousy. The emotional situation provides a means of presenting wider issues of human life. It is true to say that the play is about appearance and reality, but that is true of most of Shakespeare's other plays, and so it does not get us very far. One of the play's main features is the very clear interplay of oppositions, and it is through them that we may come to a fuller understanding of its fundamental concerns.

3.1.1 Black and white

Shakespeare takes as his protagonist a black man. Though he is called a Moor, which might seem to indicate to us a brown-skinned man of Arab race, as late as the seventeenth century Moors were assumed to be mostly black. It is clear from the text of Othello that Shakespeare did not see his tragic hero as brown-skinned. Roderigo's reference to him as 'the thick lips' (I. i. 66), Iago's description of him as 'an old black ram', and Othello's own words, 'Haply for I am black . . . ' (III. iii. 260) indicate a character with negroid features, and one who is therefore much more distinctly different from a European than an Arab would be. The sharpness of contrast is emphasised not only by Iago in his image of the 'old black ram' tupping the 'white ewe' but also it is clear in other ways that Shakespeare wants his audience to have a strong sense of Othello's blackness. From the evidence of the presentation of other black characters in the plays of the period, it would appear likely that the contemporary audience would have expected the black man to have been evil, or at least lascivious and brutal. Black was the colour associated with the devil in a commonly-accepted system of colour symbolism, whereas its opposite, white, represented purity and goodness, and this colour symbolism was applied somewhat irrationally to skin pigmentation. Othello does not appear in the first scene of the play, and he is not referred to by name within it, only as 'the Moor'. Audience preconceptions about Moors would have meant that Iago's references to the 'black ram' and the 'Barbary horse', and the making of the beast with two backs, as well as Roderigo's reference to 'the gross clasps of a lascivious Moor' (I. i. 127) would probably not have seemed as extreme and possibly wide of the truth as they would to a present-day audience more sensitive to racial prejudice. Although there are indications to the audience in the first scene that the view which is being presented of the Moor may be biased and inaccurate, the animal references and the suggestions of lasciviousness and sexual potency correspond to the characteristics of the popular Elizabethan stereotype.

What Shakespeare does in the second scene, in which Othello appears for the first time, is to overturn preconceptions, presenting a man who is the exact opposite of the stereotype, not an animal but a noble human being, whose qualities raise him above the white characters we have so far seen in the play, a man calm and in control in contrast to Brabantio's emotional fury, a man of integrity and openness in contrast to Iago's deviousness, and a man whom love has truly moved and transformed, as opposed to the superficial and weak Roderigo. By presenting a man who, though outwardly black, possesses, in terms of moral colour symbolism, inner whiteness of character, Shakespeare subverts audience expectations and develops a questioning frame of mind which the first scene has already established in other ways (see Chapter 2). In this case it is a questioning of appearances, and contrasts between appearance and reality are at the very heart of the play, with Iago as the character in whom those contrasts are most sharply focused. Shakespeare's presentation of the black Othello raises the question, 'Who, in moral terms, is the black man and who is the white man?' It is the white-skinned Iago who is the villain but who is believed throughout to be honest, and, as the Duke says to Brabantio, referring to Othello, 'Your son-in-law is far more fair than black' (I. iii. 288). Shakespeare forces his audience to shed superficial stereotyping, to think about individuals, and to see that it is inner character, truth and values which matter. However, because he is concerned with presenting not stereotypes but complex human beings, Shakespeare does not deal in simple black and white contrasts, though we can obviously make some. Shakespeare both rejects the stereotype and yet suggests there may be some grain of truth in it. Othello does possess the passion and the potential for savagery which are features of the stereotype, for it is these forces which Iago's poison releases, and which are expressed in lines such as 'I'll tear her all to pieces!' (III. iii. 426) and 'I will chop her into messes!' (IV. i. 210). It is Iago's evil which in fact reduces the noble Othello to the stereotype, destroying the very individual characteristics which raise him above it, and transforming his inner whiteness to blackness. When this happens, his vision of the world is transformed, and apart from Iago he ceases to think 'men honest that but seem to be so'. Shakespeare's play with the idea of the blackness of Othello's skin and his inner whiteness is developed as he believes Desdemona to be unfaithful to him: fair becomes black, and Othello expresses this in words which refer to his name having become as black as his face (III. iii. 382–4). Some editions of the play read 'Her name' rather than 'My name' at this point, but in both cases the idea of transformation is implied. If the lines refer to Desdemona's name, they clearly underline the success of Iago's plan which was to 'turn her virtue into pitch'.

However, at the opening of the final scene, Othello's words stress again the whiteness of Desdemona's skin, a whiteness which is superlative, and which reminds us again of her untainted inner whiteness just before she is to die an innocent victim – 'Yet I'll not shed her blood,/Nor scar that whiter skin of hers than snow' (V. ii. 3–4).

3.1.2 Darkness and light

The black/white contrasts are complemented by contrasts between darkness and light. Three out of five acts take place at night or when a storm darkens the skies. The whole of the first act takes place at night. At the opening of the play Shakespeare does not draw the attention of the audience to the fact for nearly seventy lines. The early dialogue of Iago and Roderigo could be taking place at any time of the day or night, but as Iago prompts Roderigo to rouse Brabantio, it is almost as if night closes in with this the first of his plans to make trouble. From line 68 the dialogue contains many details (90, 99, 124, 141–5, 168, 183) which create and sustain a sense of night and darkness, beginning with Iago's vivid simile –

> Do, with like timorous accent and dire yell
> As when, by night and negligence, the fire
> Is spied in populous cities. (75–7) –

full of suggestions of danger and impending disaster. It was popularly believed that night was the time when the devil was chiefly at work and witchcraft was practised. Shakespeare subtly connects Iago with the darkness. Also, the night setting gives more credibility to Iago's association of Othello with the devil and with the nightmare images of the young girl being 'covered with a Barbary horse' and of 'the beast with two backs'.

Iago's own association with night and darkness, with the suggestions of evil practice and deception (darkness hiding truth), is emphasised further at the end of the act as he thinks of a plan – 'Hell and night/Must bring this monstrous birth to the world's light.' The next scene immediately opens with a storm, and the dramatic effect is almost to suggest that by some act of witchcraft Iago has conjured it up.

The night scenes of the first act are scenes of hurried activity, comings and goings, uncertainties, threats and confusion. The darkness of night provides an emblem of the difficulty characters have in getting at the truth; Brabantio at first does not believe Roderigo and Iago; the Senate does not know what to believe from the conflicting reports of Turkish movements; and the Duke is determined to get at the truth of Brabantio's accusations against Othello. The confusions of Act I are resolved only to be followed by the storm, but the darkness of Act V is much thicker: in the first scene Cassio is wounded and Roderigo is killed by Iago who, ironically, is the only person with a light, and who moves in the darkness as if it were his natural element, the only character who knows clearly what is happening. The other characters are in a state of confusion, and the dialogue stresses this. Again darkness acts as a symbol of the situation Iago has created in which the truth is totally obscured, but by this stage the darkness and confusion are much more intense and complete than they were in Act I. At the beginning of the play the commanding integrity of Othello was sufficient to prevent the truth being obscured, but by the end that integrity has been undermined.

It is perhaps one of the play's supreme ironies that the undermining by deception occurs not in one of the scenes of darkness but in the daylight of Acts III and IV, when Othello is able to observe Cassio in conversation with Iago and with Bianca, and thinks what he sees is evidence to support his suspicions. Just as he presents a black man who is in fact 'white', and a lying villain whom everyone believes to be honest, so Shakespeare also presents the greatest deception taking place in a daylight scene when Othello thinks he can see things clearly.

We may see a dimension of the light/dark contrast in the imagery which Othello is given. His speeches in the earlier part of the play present wide views of the world, a sense of the open air, of colour, and of distance, sometimes expressed in terms of spatial contrasts of depth and height, for example

Rough quarries, rocks, and hills whose heads touch heaven

(I. iii. 140)

and

> And let the labouring bark climb hills of seas
> Olympus-high, and duck again as low
> As hell's from heaven. (II. i. 185–7)

When Iago's mental poison begins to take effect images of restriction, stagnation, ugliness and darkness enter Othello's speeches. The open views give way to the image of the toad in the dark well (III. iii. 267–8; IV. ii. 60–1).

The contrast between darkness and light is powerfully present at the opening of the final scene. The first visual impression is of the entry of Othello into the darkened bedroom with a flaming torch. One effect of this is to establish a connection with Iago in the previous scene who had been the only figure in the darkness who carried a light, thus suggesting on one level that Othello at this stage is a reflection of Iago intent upon the destruction of goodness. On another level the image serves to underline the self-image Othello projects in his speech, seeing himself as an agent of justice and truth punishing sin and deception. The conflicting and complex emotions of this speech are conveyed by a third level of significance which is given to the image of light. Desdemona, or life *in* Desdemona, is presented as a light which cannot be relit once it has been extinguished. The act of killing her will be like putting out a light forever. The inner conflict is revealed through the association of Desdemona at one moment with the blackness of sin which must be punished by Othello as moral light-bearer, and at the next with light itself, Othello's action bringing darkness.

3.1.3 Angel and devil: Heaven and Hell

When Othello admits to Emilia in the last scene that he has killed Desdemona, she cries 'Oh, the more angel she,/And you the blacker devil!' (V. ii. 132–3). This contrast between the forces of good and evil is one which is made throughout the play. Emilia's words suggest that Othello has become a devil, and we recall that in the earlier part of the play it is Iago who is associated with the devil and hell. Though he tries to suggest to Brabantio in the first scene that Othello is associated with the forces of evil – 'the devil will make a grandsire of you' – the final soliloquy of the first act links Iago himself with hell and night, and a later soliloquy in II. iii strengthens this connection:

> Divinity of hell!
> When devils will the blackest sins put on,
> They do suggest at first with heavenly shows,
> As I do now. (II. iii. 361–4)

The nature of evil is characterised by false appearances which are used to entrap the victim, and such is Iago's chief characteristic. When Emilia refers to Othello in the last scene as a devil our attention is drawn to the fact that Iago has transformed and made him like himself through his evil suggestions.

As the soliloquy in II. iii. indicates, it is Iago's intention to transform all that is good and beautiful to evil and ugliness. He will use Desdemona's generous and compassionate nature to destroy her and Othello's love for her –

> I'll pour this pestilence into his ear –
> That she repeals him for her body's lust;
> And by how much she strives to do him good
> She shall undo her credit with the Moor.
> So will I turn her virtue to pitch,
> And out of her own goodness make the net
> That shall enmesh them all. (II. iii. 367–73)

One of the ways in which Shakespeare points the success of Iago's plan is through the use of the angel/devil contrast. By the end of the great temptation scene (III. iii.) Othello refers to Desdemona as 'the fair devil'. She has been transformed in his mind. In the next scene he talks of 'a young and sweating devil' in her hand (III. iv. 42). As he collapses in incoherence in IV. i, he cries 'Oh devil!' (44). When he strikes Desdemona in public in the same scene, Othello calls her 'devil' three times. In IV. ii he says 'Heaven knows thou art as false as hell', and presents Emilia as the keeper of the gate of hell (89–91). Earlier in the play Desdemona and her relationship with Othello have been presented as connected with heaven. To Cassio she is 'The divine Desdemona' (II. i. 73) who comes through the storm like a goddess before whom the dangerous seas and rocks give way and cease to threaten. As she arrives, Cassio presents her as having a divine protection:

> Hail to thee, lady, and the grace of heaven,
> Before, behind thee, and on every hand,
> Enwheel thee round! (II. i. 85–7)

To Othello, reunited with his wife after the storm, she is his 'soul's joy', and he uses a contrast of heaven and hell to contrast this moment of happiness with the separation in the storm. Desdemona replies by praying for heaven's blessing on their love,

> The heavens forbid
> But that our loves and comforts should increase
> Even as our days do grow. (II. i. 192–4)

These lines associate their love with growth and creativity, a connection which is made elsewhere in the play. When at III. iii. 90–2 Othello expresses his love for Desdemona,

> Perdition catch my soul
> But I do love thee! And when I love thee not
> Chaos is come again

he connects that love with the love of God which is the motivating force of creation, when the world was created out of chaos and darkness and God said 'Let there be light'. Earlier Iago associates Desdemona with generosity expressed as fruitfulness, 'She's framed as fruitful/As the free elements'. As goddess, angel and loving creature, she is the opposite of Iago's devilry and his destructive nature. When he realises what he has done in killing the innocent woman and in destroying all that he held most dear, Othello has a vision of himself in hell being tormented by the devils (V. ii. 278–80).

The linked contrasts of black and white, darkness and light, heaven and hell, indicate that the tragedy is not conceived simply as a limited domestic tragedy of a jealous husband who murders his wife, but as an emblem of a universal conflict between larger forces of good and evil, of creation and negation, life and death, love and hatred. The language and poetry, particularly of Othello himself, help to provide perspectives which make us look beyond the domestic world to the wider world of distant places, heroic action, and the elemental forces of nature.

3.1.4 Christian and Turk

By placing the personal story of Othello and Desdemona against a background of public events and conflicts with which Othello himself is closely connected, Shakespeare provides another means of relating it to wider issues. The conflict between Christian Venice and the Turks is used as another way of presenting the clash between forces of good and evil. The Turks, who were, even in Shakespeare's day, seen as an armed Muslim threat to Christian Europe, are associated in the play with deceptive appearance (for example, they pretend to have designs on Rhodes whereas their real target is Cyprus; I. iii.), and with destruction, even fighting among themselves as Othello suggests (II. iii. 174–6). Their characteristics are easily seen as a reflection of those exemplified by Iago, and Shakespeare underlines this by putting into his own mouth words which connect him with the Turk, whilst playfully denying that connection – 'Nay, it is true, or else I am a Turk' (II. i. 114). If Iago is the white man who is really 'black', he is also the Christian who is really a 'Turk', and Othello, whose origins as a pagan are at times stressed, is by contrast more clearly possessed of Christian qualities. The Turks were regarded by the Elizabethans as the infidel, the enemies of the true faith. Like them, Iago sets out to undermine the faith and trust upon which the relationship of Othello and Desdemona rests.

3.2 IMPORTANT ISSUES OF INTERPRETATION

3.2.1 Why does Iago do it?

When he is finally unmasked as a villain in the last scene of the play, Iago refuses to answer Othello's question, 'Why hath he thus ensnared my soul and body?' (301), resolutely announcing, 'Demand me nothing. What you know, you know/From this time forth I never will speak word' (302–3). During the play Shakespeare provides different suggestions and clues, particularly in Iago's own speeches, about his motivation, but we remain uncertain what to accept and are unable confidently to provide a simple reason for his actions. Iago's refusal in the final scene to give Othello an explanation is also Shakespeare's refusal to provide one for the audience. We are left with a sense of the unknowable and mysterious nature of his evil, and if, as has been suggested in the previous section, the action of the play is not limited to the domestic dimension but presents a cosmic conflict in which Iago is connected with a universal force of evil, then it is clear that Shakespeare would not have wanted to reduce his motivation simply to that of a man who has failed to gain promotion and who intends to get his own back on those who have slighted him.

A certain mystery surrounds Iago, but there are observations which we can make, and though we may not be able fully to explain him, yet he provides the clearest indication of the nature of evil in the play. We have to be careful when examining the motives he ascribes to himself. When he says in the first scene that he hates Othello for his pride and arbitrary nature in promoting an inexperienced man like Cassio and failing to give his own worth and service due recognition, we should perhaps be sceptical about whether these facts, if indeed they are true, provide the key to his actions later. Iago presents this motive to Roderigo, a character he is manipulating and deceiving, and the veracity of his words must be in doubt. Furthermore, we are quickly made aware that Iago is a person whose words and actions often disguise his real thoughts and intentions. He is not a character who can be trusted, and certainly not when he is talking to others. What he says in soliloquy is another matter. The soliloquy, spoken by a character alone on stage, provides us directly with the character's thoughts. We can place more reliance on the truth of what is said. Yet can we be sure in Iago's case? If we look at his soliloquy at the end of the first act, we find another motive suggested: revenge

against Othello for seducing Emilia. This is interesting because the
motive is jealousy, precisely the emotion Iago sets out to stir up in
Othello. It does seem that some credence can be given to this as an
explanation as in his next soliloquy, at the end of II. i, Iago describes
the thought of his wife's infidelity gnawing at him 'like a poisonous
mineral'. The image is strong; the force of gnawing suggests the
painfulness of this thought constantly with him. However, the Act I
soliloquy does not allow us the certainty that this is a full or adequate
explanation of motive. Iago admits that he has no proof that there is
any truth in the rumour, yet he is still determined to exact a revenge.
His words are revealing –

> I hate the Moor,
> And it is thought abroad that 'twixt my sheets
> He's done my office.

Notice that he does not say 'it is thought that Othello has been to bed
with my wife and I hate him for it'. The '*And* it is thought', placed as
it is, suggests that the rumour is not the reason for the hatred, but a
factor which bolsters an already-existing antagonism. The mention of
the rumour seems more like an attempt to provide an understandable
explanation for an inexplicable hatred, an attempt at rationalisation.
The flimsiness of this explanation is revealed not only by the fact that
Iago has no proof, but also by his description of Othello later in the
speech as of 'a free and open nature', the kind of man who clearly
would not stoop to the sort of deception and underhand action with
Emilia of which Iago supposedly suspects him. This is not to say that
we should reject jealousy as a motive since his Act II, scene i
soliloquy refers again forcefully to it, but that we should be wary of
assuming it is the sole motive.

We may gain fuller understanding of Iago if we look elsewhere in
the play. With Roderigo at the end of I. iii, and at the end of II. i,
Iago presents the relationship of Othello and Desdemona as entirely
physical, as lust, not a love which has any depth or spiritual
dimension. He says that he is sure that both partners are changeable
and will grow tired of each other – 'She must change for youth: when
she is sated with his body she will find the errors of her choice' (I. iii.
352–4). He seems to deny that love or virtue exist in the world. He is,
of course, saying this to Roderigo whom he is deceiving, and careful
consideration should prevent us from taking his words entirely at
their face value. Elsewhere, in his soliloquies he does acknowledge
that Desdemona is good and virtuous, and says that he will turn her
virtue 'into pitch'. He also acknowledges that Othello has noble
qualities and that 'he'll prove to Desdemona/A most dear husband'
(II. i. 294–5), which suggests that he does not believe what he says to
Roderigo. There seems, however, to be a certain relish on his part at

seeing the Othello/Desdemona relationship as merely physical and lustful, which is in accord with the obvious relish he has in describing their love-making in animal terms to Brabantio in the first scene. What this perhaps suggests is that though he knows the natures of Othello and Desdemona are not as he describes them to Brabantio and Roderigo he wishes they were like that: he would like their love simply to be a physical matter, lacking depth and an enduring quality.

Why should this be so? There is a revealing comment in V. i, when Iago says of Cassio, 'He hath a daily beauty in his life/That makes me ugly' (V. i, 19–20). This suggests that there may be more to his desire to destroy Cassio than simply the fact that Cassio was promoted over him. If being passed over by Othello for the lieutenancy was indeed a slight to his worth and experience as a soldier, the comments here suggest that Cassio has qualities which Iago does not possess, and that his very presence makes the ensign aware of his own deficiencies as a person. Iago's cynical comments to Roderigo, to Desdemona in II. i, and to Cassio on reputation in II. iii, suggest a man who has not experienced the overwhelming love which Othello and Desdemona have for each other and who has no sense of spiritual being. All the evidence suggests that the relationship between Iago and his wife, Emilia, is unsatisfactory (see Section 4.1.4) and just as he may wish to destroy Cassio because his presence makes him aware of his own deficiencies, so too, perhaps, he wishes to destroy the relationship of Othello and Desdemona because it makes him intensely aware of what he does not have. His first plan in rousing Brabantio is to prevent Othello from enjoying the happiness he has found; he intends to

> poison his delight
> . . . .
> . . . .
> Plague him with flies. Though that his joy be joy,
> Yet throw such chances of vexation on't
> As it may lose some colour. (I. i. 68, 71–73)

He enjoys disturbing Brabantio's peace of mind, too, as he later enjoys disturbing Cassio with the reminder that Desdemona is in bed with Othello at the opening of II. iii, and as more fully he enjoys the destruction of Othello's own peace of mind from III. iii onwards. Iago's second and third soliloquies which emphasise his jealous suspicions, and present that jealousy gnawing at him, suggests a mind that is not at peace, and the indications are that he desires to make others like himself. Shakespeare seems to confirm this by indicating in a number of ways that the change which takes place in Othello as a result of the jealousy makes him more like Iago. This is reflected for instance in the imagery and in the two scenes of Act V in which Iago and Othello are torchbearers. The effect of Iago's poison is to reduce the noble Moor to the savage and to the popular stereotype, but also to bring him down to Iago's level of fevered sexual imagining and cynical comment, for example, on Emilia as a bawd, IV. ii. 19–20. Such a view makes Iago's evil not motiveless, not simply a desire to act in a destructive way for the sake of it, but the desire to create a world in which everyone is like Iago himself, and where he need no longer feel deficient and an outsider. Such a view, too, points another irony, in that one of the ways Iago undermines Othello is by making him feel the outsider (the Moor who does not know the ways of Venetian women; the African in a white European society), whereas the view that has been presented here suggests that it is Iago himself who is the real outsider.

It must be emphasised that this is only one way of making sense of the character, an interpretation which might be countered by other possible interpretations simply because Shakespeare provides us not with definitive explanations but with suggestions and insights, which we may interpret, as the critics have, in various ways in order to reach a view of Iago and his evil. Any interpretation needs to try to take into consideration all the evidence, to assess the nature and value of different kinds of evidence, and to reach a view that is coherent. But when we have done that a certain mystery may still remain because Shakespeare has not told us what to think.

3.2.2 The problem of Othello

The first half of the play
Critics have been very much divided in their views of the character of Othello. There are those like A. C. Bradley, Helen Gardner, and Juliet McLauchlan, who stress the character's nobility, whilst others, most notably F. R. Leavis, take a distinctly anti-heroic view, presenting Othello as self-dramatising and self-deluding (see Chapter 6 'Critical Reception', and 'Further Reading'). You need to be aware that such very different interpretations are possible and, when you have a thorough knowledge of the text itself, you may find it useful to read the contributions by Bradley and Gardner on the one side and Eliot and Leavis on the other which are printed in the *Othello* volume in the Macmillan Casebook series. You should be aware that the scene by scene commentary in this Master Guide presents an interpretation which rejects the anti-heroic view.

We should take account of the fact that almost every character in the play, including Iago himself in his private moments, acknowledges Othello's nobility or greatness of spirit. Even Brabantio thought well enough of him to invite him to his house frequently, and towards the end of the play Lodovico reminds us of what the

general opinion of Othello had been as he expresses amazement at
the public striking and humiliation of Desdemona:

> Is this the noble Moor whom our full senate
> Call all in all sufficient? Is this the nature
> Whom passion could not shake? Whose solid virtue
> The shot of accident nor dart of chance
> Could neither graze nor pierce? (IV. i. 274–8)

Is everyone deceived in Othello as they are in Iago? We should
perhaps pay attention to the effect Shakespeare creates by the
appearance of Othello in I. ii after Iago's view of him has been
presented in the previous scene. The juxtaposition helps to justify
acceptance of Othello's nobility, particularly seen in terms of his
openness, honesty, courage, calm assurance and authority. He
appears to have a just, rather than an inflated, sense of his own
worth. One of his main characteristics is his calmness and control in
the first half of the play. Othello is so sure of himself, of the rightness
of his actions, and of the worth of the love which he and Desdemona
share, but Shakespeare does nothing to make us question all this in
the first part of the play. Othello clearly does possess authority, not
just because the Senate invests him with it, but as an intrinsic part of
his personality, springing from sureness of himself and of his view of
the world. He shows it in Act I and again in Act II when the
extremely important brawl scene (II. iii.) shows his calmness on the
verge of being shaken by anger as one person after another refuses or
fails to give an explanation of what has taken place. Iago undermines
Othello's calmness and rationality by stirring up his 'blood', that is,
his passions, anger, jealousy, hatred, which overwhelm him. He does
so by undermining not only Othello's vision of Desdemona but, in so
doing, his vision of himself, for Othello's love for his wife is so great
that he sees her as a source of his own life:

> But there where I have garnered up my heart,
> Where either I must live or bear no life,
> The fountain from the which my current runs
> Or else dries up. (IV. ii. 56–9)

That Othello has a self-image does not automatically make him
self-dramatizing or insincere: it is a necessary condition of mental
health that we believe in ourselves and our own worth, and mental
breakdown and madness often arise from circumstances in which a
person's self-image is destroyed or undermined. The first half of the
play suggests that Othello's self-image corresponds with the person
we actually see him to be, and acknowledged to be by most of the
other characters. To see him otherwise is to see him as Iago would

like to see him. To question the worth of the love of Othello and Desdemona is also to adopt the cynical view of Iago's conversations with Roderigo. But Iago's own words in his soliloquies indicate that he does not really believe this, and, after all, there would be nothing tragic in the fall of an arrogant man and the destruction of a superficial relationship.

A line which is often quoted and has been used to indicate the kind of self-approving self-dramatisation of which Leavis accuses Othello, is the line in I. ii, in which he prevents conflict between Brabantio's followers and his own, 'Keep up your bright swords, for the dew will rust them' (I. ii. 59). The image is indeed vivid and striking but Leavis, I believe, misses the presence of an element of wit in the line by which Othello attempts to defuse the situation. It is a piece of exaggeration to suggest that the swords will become rusty simply by being unsheathed for this conflict, but by this exaggeration Othello implies to the people around him that it is ridiculous to fight. The contrast, too, between the 'bright swords' and the rusted swords also gives the line a moral dimension by suggesting that to fight over such a matter would be dishonourable – the bright swords which should be used to defend honour and true worth will be tarnished by being used in this case. Seen in these ways the line adds to our appreciation of Othello's character as authoritative, noble and morally clear-sighted.

We also have to be careful of looking at the speeches of Othello as if they were the utterances of a living person. If we do that we may well feel they are self-dramatising. The speeches are given to the character by the dramatist who uses them to convey more than simply features of character. To say that Othello's poetic utterance indicates his self-approving self-dramatising tendency is to fail to take into account the effects created by Shakespeare's use of language and his technique of juxtaposition (see Chapter 4). For instance, look at II. i, the arrival in Cyprus, and consider the effect of the juxtaposition of Iago's cynical prose comments on women when he speaks to Desdemona and Emilia, and Othello's poetic greeting of his wife. If Othello's poetry is intended to convey self-delusion, then presumably we are meant to accept, by comparison and juxtaposition, that Iago presents a 'true' view of the world – to accept him as 'honest Iago' in fact, with his blunt down-to-earth manner. But this is contrary to the actual effect of the scene in the theatre. The audience responds to the poetry, to *Shakespeare's* rhetoric, and as Othello and Desdemona greet each other the audience becomes aware of another level of experience beside which Iago's view of the world seems hollow and shoddy. The fact that Iago cannot speak as Othello speaks is a clue to our understanding of the nature of his evil (see Section 3.2).

The second half of the play
It is perhaps the second half of the play from III. iii onwards which

creates the problems, and in trying to answer them commentators sometimes distort interpretation of Othello's character in the first half of the play when it is actually quite clearly defined. The first major problem is the great 'temptation scene', III. iii. Does Shakespeare strain our credibility to present us within a single scene with a change from an Othello who says, early on,

> Perdition catch my soul
> But I do love thee! And when I love thee not
> Chaos is come again.   (90–2)

to one who ends calling Desdemona 'lewd minx' and 'devil', and crying 'Oh, damn her!/Damn her'? Or does Shakespeare wish us to gather from this change that Othello is excessively gullible, and that he is a much weaker character than we thought him to be? You might first consider how rapid the change actually is. This is the longest scene in the play, and Othello's soliloquy breaks it into two parts, making it more like two scenes than one. Othello does not change from absolute love to sudden absolute distrust at one moment. The scenes which follow III. iii show the growth of jealousy. What Shakespeare does not make clear is when exactly in this scene Othello begins to feel the first hints of jealousy. You need to ask yourself at what point you think a change begins to occur and why, and then to consider to what extent Shakespeare makes this credible by having adequately prepared for it. If you look at the Commentary on this scene, you will see that it suggests that Iago's attack on Othello's mind and emotions is very carefully structured so that one thing builds upon another; he establishes his ground before advancing, going step by step and observing Othello's reactions in order to judge when he can take advantage of weakness or when it is safe to say more. This careful structuring of the deception helps us to see why it works successfully and thus helps to make Othello's reaction more credible.

Iago relies on Othello's belief in his honesty. If this shows Othello's gullibility, then everyone else in the play is equally gullible, for Othello is not the only person to believe him to be trustworthy. Act II, scene iii provides a good illustration of how Iago creates this appearance – Cassio, Montano and Othello all believe he is a trustworthy character as a result of his behaviour in this scene. Othello's trust in Iago is, therefore, surely not incredible. Iago plays upon differences of social background as a means of unsettling Othello, suggesting to him that he, Iago, knows Venice and Venetian women better than his master. He makes Othello feel an outsider, at an obvious disadvantage in judging the situation. He then follows it up with a reference to what Othello knows to be true, that Desdemona deceived her father. (You should consider with each of Iago's ploys why he introduces them into the conversation at the point he does.) Othello, it appears, has no previous experience of love and his relationship with Desdemona has been of such short duration that he lacks the resources of experience to counter the suggestions of one who by his apparent honesty and loyalty, and by being a Venetian, has strong claims to be believed.

The double time-scheme
But surely, we might ask, Othello must see through Iago's deception because there has been no time for Desdemona to be unfaithful with Cassio. He did not even travel on the same ship to Cyprus, and the 'temptation scene' seems to be taking place on the day after the arrival on the island. Critics have noted that the play has a double time sequence. The time sequence suggested from the beginning of Act II is of about two to three days, the arrival in Cyprus, the night of the brawl which follows it, the next day and the following night, with clear references made in the text to times of the day. Othello's instruction to Iago at the end of III. iii, to murder Cassio within three days, suggests a slightly longer period for the action than two days but still a short one. This time scheme gives the play dramatic intensity but it also creates the problem that the alleged adultery between Desdemona and Cassio could not have taken place. Yet there are other references which suggest a longer time scheme; for instance, Emilia says that Iago had 'a hundred times' tried to persuade her to steal Desdemona's handkerchief, and Bianca accuses Cassio of not visiting her for a whole week. These time discrepancies, whilst being fairly evident when we study the text of the play, are much less noticeable as a problem when we see the play performed. In fact the longer time suggestions help to make more credible the deception of Othello by Iago, whilst the shorter time references contribute to dramatic intensity, but are themselves also necessary for credibility as Iago's deceptions would surely have been detected over a longer period of time.

Othello's final speech

> Speak of me as I am: nothing extenuate,
> Nor set down aught in malice. Then must you speak
> Of one that loved, not wisely, but too well;
> Of one not easily jealous, but being wrought,
> Perplexed in the extreme. (V. ii. 341–5)

Is this an example of Othello's self-delusion? Was he really 'not easily jealous'? Your view of the speech will depend upon your interpretation of III. iii, and of the stages of Othello's jealousy. If you feel that in that scene the change in Othello was rather incredible then you will probably not agree with the estimate of himself in his final speech, but will see him as being quite the opposite, easily jealous. The Commentary in Chapter 2 of this book suggests a progression within the final scene from Othello's first speech in which he tries to assume the role of impersonal agent of justice; through the 'Behold I have a weapon' speech in which he tries to resume the role of heroic soldier fighting his way out of a tight corner, but comes to see this kind of action as futile and hollow in view of Desdemona's death, so that he realises acceptance of the punishment and of the torment of hell is the only course which can have any meaning for him; to, finally, the last speech in which he kills the 'Turk' that he himself has become. This interpretation presents his final speech not as a speech of self-delusion, but of self-recognition and understanding. His course of action is not to fight his way out of the room but to kill the evil in himself. He begins the scene as a false agent of justice intent on killing the innocent Desdemona, but he ends as a true agent of justice killing his guilty self.

The final speech has been a source of much critical controversy. Whatever view you hold of it should depend on how you view Othello's character, his words and actions, in earlier parts of the play.

4 TECHNICAL FEATURES

4.1 JUXTAPOSITION

The first part of Chapter 3 looked at the way in which the play is built upon a number of oppositions or antitheses, darkness and light, black and white, devil and angel, Turk and Christian. When we look at the technical features of the play we are looking at the means by which the themes and issues are presented and articulated. A major technique which we find in Shakespeare's work as a whole is juxtaposition, or setting one thing against another for purposes of contrast, comparison or connection. Juxtaposition may be of various kinds.

4.1.1 One part of a scene set against another part

A good example of this is II. i. in which Cassio's speeches about Desdemona before she enters are set against the dialogue between Desdemona and Iago that follows, which itself is set against Othello's reunion with his wife. What characterises Cassio's speeches is a reverence for Desdemona as a creature of spiritual worth. This is set against the cynicism of Iago's speeches about women, which presents a contrast to Othello and Desdemona's expression of their love in terms of high poetry, linking it to the divine order. The juxtapositioning of these parts of the scene establishes tonal contrasts; the wonder and awe of Cassio, Othello and Desdemona, set against the cynically critical and denigratory tone of Iago which is continued in the subsequent section with Roderigo. Such tonal juxtaposition helps to convey the thematic contrasts of the play and provides us with a feeling of the antithetical views of life they express.

4.1.2 Verse and prose

These tonal contrasts are achieved partly through juxtapositioning of verse and prose within the scene. Cassio and Othello speak in blank verse. The dialogue of Iago with Desdemona is in a mixture of prose and banal rhyming verse (for example, 147–59) as Iago presents his view of women, while his later dialogue with Roderigo is entirely in prose. Prose does not involve a regular rhythmic structure and is therefore like ordinary speech, whereas verse, though it can in the hands of a skilful writer like Shakespeare suggest speech patterns, has intensity and resonance as a result of the pointed significance of words, phrases and images within a formal structure. Although we may not be consciously aware of the change from prose to blank verse in the theatre, we shall probably respond subconsciously to the heightened quality of the language when that change is made. In II. i the blank verse of Cassio and Othello is characterised by sentences which are spread over several lines, so that we have to wait for their completion to understand their full meaning. This gives the speeches weight and dignity, as does the building of phrase upon phrase in Cassio's first speech, for instance, 'Tempests themselves, high seas, and howling winds,/The guttered rocks and congregated sands. . .' (II. i. 68–9). In contrast to these effects, Iago's rhyming couplets as he speaks about women sound false and empty because of their jingling and obvious rhymes, for example:

> She that was ever fair, and never proud,
> Had tongue at will, and yet was never loud,
> Never lacked gold, and yet went never gay,
> Fled from her wish, and yet said 'Now I may',. . . (147–50)

There is a building of clause upon clause here with repetition of the word 'never', and we wait for the conclusion of this catalogue, but the rhymes convey a tone of mockery and denigration. You can find examples of the juxtaposition of verse and prose elsewhere in the play.

4.1.3 One scene juxtaposed to another

An obvious example of how this is used is the first two scenes of the play. If you think carefully about it, you will realise that as far as the story he had to tell was concerned, there were many ways in which Shakespeare could have begun his play. He did not have to begin with the scene he gives us. For instance, he could have begun with the Senate scene (I. iii.), which provides us with most of the background to the story of Othello and Desdemona's love; or with Act II, scene i, omitting the Venice scenes altogether, as Guiseppe Verdi did when, in the nineteenth century, he wrote his opera, *Otello*, based on Shake-speare's tragedy. You might well consider the effects of such alternat-ive openings. In the play as we actually have it, we are provided in the

64

first scene with a view of Othello through Iago's eyes, which is then juxtaposed to the view of the character we receive directly when he appears in the second scene. Such a juxtaposition encourages an active and analytical frame of mind in the audience by making us put one set of impressions against another. We are here made highly aware of the deception of Iago and the contrasts between appearance and reality with which the play is concerned. If the play began with the present third scene we should have lost the insights into Iago, and the clarity of perspective which Scene 2 set against Scene 1 provides to enable us to appreciate the ironies and to see clearly what is happening in Scene 3.

4.1.4 Contrasts between sets of relationships

Shakespeare contrasts the relationships of Othello and Desdemona, Iago and Emilia, and Cassio and Bianca as a means of developing audience understanding of the play's central concerns. The latter two relationships provide contrasts with, and comments on, the first.

Iago and Emilia
Shakespeare provides suggestions about the relationship but does not give direct comment or description. The evidence suggests that it is not a satisfactory or happy marriage. Iago's soliloquies in I, iii and II, i reveal that he has suspicions, though no proof, of Emilia's infidelity with Othello, and he describes his jealousy 'like a poisonous mineral' that gnaws him inwardly. Earlier in II. i his cynical and mocking words about his wife suggest that she is a scold and that their household is one of domestic discord. When Cassio greets Emilia with a kiss, Iago says

> Sir, would she give you so much of her lips
> As of her tongue she oft bestows on me,
> You would have enough. (II.i. 101–3).

Emilia protests that this is not true, but then Iago goes on to suggest that it is true of all women who are

>   pictures out of door;
> Bells in your parlours, wildcats in your kitchens;
> Saints in your injuries, devils being offended;
> Players in your housewifery, and housewives in your beds.
>   (II. i. 109–12)

The lines suggest that there is a great difference between women's public appearances and what they are actually like at home. It is noticeable that Emilia does not protest again, except to say that she will not look to her husband for praise, and remains silent during the ensuing dialogue. Does she do so nursing hidden anger, maintaining a public appearance or propriety, but waiting to give vent to her anger when they are alone together, thus proving Iago's point? Or does she remain silent because she is hurt? The incident with the handkerchief in III. iii provides further suggestions. Emilia knows how important the dropped handkerchief is to Desdemona, but she decides to keep it in order to give it to her husband 'to please his fantasy'. Iago has apparently asked her a hundred times to obtain it for him, and will presumably be pleased with her. This is perhaps the action of a woman whose husband is cold towards her and who is trying to win back his love and regard by giving him something she knows that he wants. Her attempt meets with no success. When Iago enters he speaks angrily, asking her what she is doing there alone, and when Emilia says 'I have a thing for you', he twists her words obscenely, suggesting his wife is sexually available to everyone. There are indications here of the jealousy and suspicions about his wife's infidelity which Iago has voiced earlier. When she shows him the handkerchief hoping to gain his favour and a kind response, he snatches it from her and refuses to tell her why he wants it. He then curtly orders her to leave. Emilia, who in all this has put her own desire for her husband's favour before duty to Desdemona, realises the futility of her action as Iago snatches the handkerchief from her, and she is immediately concerned about her mistress. Shakespeare does not provide proof of Emilia's motivation in this incident through an aside or explanation in her brief soliloquy, but only suggestions which have to be put together with the other evidence. In the next scene, when Othello has demanded the handkerchief from Desdemona, Emilia comments bitterly that Othello is jealous and

> 'Tis not a year or two shows us a man.
> They are but stomachs, and we all but food;
> They eat us hungerly, and when they are full
> They belch us. (III. iv. 99–102)

Emilia's words on men remind us of Iago's cynical comments on women in II. i. The physical imagery is both disgusting and expressive of disgust and disillusion. It is the kind of imagery which Iago himself uses. We can perhaps assume that these disillusioned sentiments spring from her own experience. This is further suggested in her words about husbands and wives in IV. iii when, in her conversation with Desdemona, she blames husbands for their wives' infidelities, and presents a view of married life as an arena of conflict, where love is non-existent and infidelity is a means of hitting back at an uncaring partner. When she speaks of husbands who 'break out in peevish jealousies,/Throwing restraint upon us' (IV. iii. 89–90) we perhaps think not only of Othello but also of Iago, who had expressed suspicion of his wife at the beginning of the play. We do not actually see him putting restraints on Emilia, but his anger at finding her alone when she offers him the handkerchief, and the order to her to leave when he has taken it, suggest he does not wish his wife to be alone or in a situation where she may be unfaithful to him. The indications are that it is Iago's jealousy which has poisoned their relationship. Despite her husband's suspicions and what Emilia herself says about the infidelity of wives, there is nothing in the text to suggest that she has actually been unfaithful. In fact the indications are that she still loves her husband in the handkerchief incident and in the final scene where she is at first incredulous as Othello tells her it was Iago who told him about Desdemona's affair with Cassio. She repeats 'My husband?' four times as if unable to believe what she has been told, but in contrast to the loving relationship and trust of Othello and Desdemona, whose love is presented as part of an harmonious divine order, the relationship of Iago and Emilia is presented as one of failure and discord.

Cassio and Bianca
This relationship is a physical one. Bianca is Cassio's mistress, and again jealousy is a significant feature, this time the jealousy of the woman rather than the man. When Cassio gives her the handkerchief to copy, Bianca immediately believes it must belong to another mistress (III. iv. 175–8). When she appears again in IV, i Bianca is even more consumed by jealousy. Cassio's attitude towards her contrasts strongly with his respect for the 'divine Desdemona'. He shows no respect or love for Bianca, laughing and mocking at her infatuation for him as he talks to Iago prior to her entrance in IV. i, just as Iago shows no respect or love for Emilia.

Shakespeare establishes connections and contrasts between the three sets of relationships by making the handkerchief important to each of them, and by presenting jealousy as a prominent feature affecting each. The relationships of Iago/Emilia and Cassio/Bianca seem to be chiefly physical in their basis. The first is soured from the start by jealousy, and, though we see less of Bianca, she becomes jealous within a few lines of her first appearance. Against these, which may seem to establish the norm for relationships in the play, the love of Othello and Desdemona has a rare and elevated quality. For him, his wife is his 'soul's joy', 'The fountain from the which [his] current runs'. Not to love her would be like the destruction of the world – 'when I love thee not/Chaos is come again'. It is the subversion of a love which is presented as so complete and absolute, and the destruction of the trust on which it is built, that is so tragic. Iago's intention is to make the relationship of Othello and Desdemona common, torn by the fears and distrust which characterise the other relationships in the play. If we look for tragic effect solely in terms of the destruction of a man of integrity and nobility, we shall miss an important dimension of the tragedy. In the love of Othello and Desdemona we are given a view of human nature which transcends the purely physical and material, and which is capable of transforming the world and of revealing the divine. What Iago destroys is the human potential for goodness and for harmony which the relationship of Othello and Desdemona expresses.

4.2 CHARACTERISATION

Juxtaposition or contrast is also a major means of characterisation in *Othello*. Language and imagery are other important means by which Shakespeare conveys to the audience an understanding of individual characters and of their place in the drama. This section will concentrate on these areas. However, Chapter 3 of this book has much to say that is relevant particularly to the characterisation of Othello and of Iago, and you may want to look back at it.

4.2.1 Character contrasts

Chapter 3 indicates how thematic concerns such as the black and white contrast are presented through contrasts between characters, particularly between Othello and Iago. There are other similar contrasts.

Roderigo and Cassio
Roderigo and Cassio are clearly different in certain respects. Iago is dismissive of the former – 'Thus do I ever make my fool my purse' (I. iii. 382), but Cassio has qualities which, for all his apparent scorn in the opening dialogue of the play, Iago has privately to acknowledge – 'He hath a daily beauty in his life/That makes me ugly' (V. i. 19–20). However, these two characters are contrasted in their responses to Desdemona. Roderigo is a type of the foolish and unsuccessful lover (he has his comic counterpart in Sir Andrew Aguecheek in Shakespeare's *Twelfth Night*) who continues to pursue his suit to win the lady's favour when it is clear that it is hopeless. Admittedly he is deceived by the insistent and persuasive Iago, who fleeces him of money and jewels, and he does at times object and appear to see through Iago's deceptions (for example, IV. ii. 171ff.), but his weakness is revealed in the relative ease with which his objections are overcome, as they are from the very first scene of the play. His attempts to 'bribe' Desdemona to respond to his advances by sending her presents through Iago associate him with mercenary attitudes, and the belief that love can be bought. However, at the

same time he protests that Desdemona is not the kind of fickle and
lascivious woman Iago tries to convince him she is. Roderigo says, 'I
cannot believe that in her – she's full of the most blessed condition'
(II. i. 249–50). Nevertheless we are given little indication that his
feelings for Desdemona have any depth or that he is genuinely
respectful towards her as Cassio is.

Iago sees that it will be plausible to suggest that Cassio, an
atttractive and refined young man, is in love with Desdemona (I. iii.
397–8). After observing Cassio's behaviour with her, Iago himself
believes there may be some truth in it, 'That Cassio loves her, I do
well believe it' (II. i. 290). Shakespeare does not indicate to the
audience whether Iago is right, but leaves us feeling that there is a
possibility that he is. Cassio's description of Desdemona coming
through the storm in II. i, is reminiscent of Elizabethan love poetry
which frequently contains imagery of ships and sea tempests. Cassio
is like the poet-lover who sees the lady as a creature to be wor-
shipped, whose beauty and virtue transform the world and provide a
vision of the divine. The poet-lover often feels the distance between
himself and this perfect woman, who seems unattainable. Sometimes
she is unattainable because she is married to someone else, as in Sir
Philip Sidney's sonnet sequence, *Astrophil and Stella*. Such, of
course, is the case of Desdemona. Cassio maintains an honourable
and respectful attitude towards her at all times, and never expresses
love for her, but what sometimes seems to be his rather weak and
rapid descent into drunkenness in II. iii, is more credible if, as the
Commentary in this book suggests, Iago tries at the beginning of the
scene to undermine Cassio by making him think of Othello making
love to Desdemona at that very moment, thus, if Cassio does secretly
love her, stirring up feelings of jealousy and loss. The strain and the
tension of maintaining an honourable and correct stance towards the
woman who has married his friend, whilst he is perhaps emotionally
in turmoil, would make Cassio's resort to drink understandable.

Desdemona and Emilia (Act IV, Scene iii)
In this scene Shakespeare presents a conversation between Desdemona and Emilia which establishes sharp contrasts of character and
attitude as a means of further emphasising the former's innocence
and virtue, and of stating again the antithesis between the demands of
love and the demands of lust. The Commentary gives a full statement
of these contrasts. We are presented with the unshakeability of
Desdemona's love, which is so great 'That even his stubbornness, his
checks, his frowns –/. . . have grace and favour' (IV. iii. 19–20). This
is set against Emilia's later speeches which suggest that the husband's
treatment of his wife is an encouragement to her to take lovers.
Desdemona expresses an attitude of absolute fidelity, whereas Emilia, though not totally immoral, states that she could be tempted and

fall if the circumstances were right. She would be prepared to be unfaithful if it meant gaining the whole world. She would not be unfaithful openly but might be so if it could be kept dark. Emilia is perhaps more like a recognisable human being, moderately moral, but capable of being tempted and falling, whilst Desdemona is clearly the ideal woman Cassio says she is. But there is something of Iago's cynicism about Emilia's speeches on married life, and one can only feel that there is a level of bitterness here which derives from her own experience of being married to him. She believes it is right to respond to hurts done to her by hurting in return, whereas Desdemona's final lines presents a different attitude, the attempt to heal rather than to hurt more.

Desdemona and Iago
Shakespeare establishes a very important contrast between Desdemona and Iago in terms of character signification. Each represents values and attitudes which are the antithesis of those held and expressed by the other. Whereas Othello as a character develops and changes, Desdemona and Iago remain the same throughout the play. This is indicative of the fact that they are used by Shakespeare to express the play's central conflict between life and anti-life forces, a conflict which has its battleground in the character of Othello. Alvin Kernan in the introduction to the Signet edition of *Othello* describes Desdemona and Iago as 'the two moral poles of the play'. He states the contrast in these terms, 'One is a life force that strives for order, community, growth, and light. The other is an anti-life force that seeks anarchy, death and darkness.'

As the foregoing comparisons of Cassio and Roderigo, and of Desdemona and Emilia have indicated, Desdemona is presented in many respects as an ideal figure of virtue. Cassio sees her as a creature of spiritual worth, coming safely through the storm like a goddess. Othello describes her as his 'soul's joy' and as the fountain, or source, of his own life. Iago acknowledges her virtue when he says that he plans to turn it into pitch. Indeed, it is Desdemona's good qualities which are the very source of her undoing. She has a concern for others, and it is her desire to help Cassio which Iago uses to convince Othello that she is in love with the former lieutenant. She shows tenderness and concern when Othello is disturbed by the first effects of Iago's mental poison, but tells his wife he is troubled by a headache. Her action in trying to soothe his brow with the handkerchief leads to her dropping it and to its being used later by Iago to fuel Othello's suspicions. Desdemona's concern for harmony and reconciliation is indicated in IV. iii, by her final words when, in contrast to Emilia, she wishes to draw good out of evil and not to produce more unhappiness by vindictively trying to hurt the husband who has hurt her. To do so would be destroy the very integrity which makes her a creature of spiritual worth. Her final act and words indicate a total selflessness as she attempts to take the blame from Othello for her death, saying she killed herself and calling her husband 'kind'. The suffering inflicted on her by Othello does not result in her love being turned to hate; her love endures even to the point of death. In IV. ii she says

> Unkindness may do much,
> And his unkindness may defeat my life,
> But never taint my love. (157–9)

Our feeling for Desdemona is heightened by the many expressions of her own sensitivity and intense feelings, for instance in her singing of the willow song in IV. iii, or in her state of shock when Othello leaves in IV. i, having accused her of being a whore. Tragic effect in this play depends upon the audience's perception of Desdemona as innocent and pure and consequently of the wrongness of Othello's perception of her as whore and devil.

Iago's character has been treated fairly fully in Chapter 3, where the matter of movitation is considered, and it is clear that he is unquestionably evil, a character who represents a spirit of negation, wishing to destroy love, virtue, trust and harmony and to turn them to their opposites. The cynical materialistic outlook which he expresses in his speeches to Roderigo, to Desdemona in II. i, and to Cassio after the brawl, stands in distinct contrast to the loving perception of spiritual values in Desdemona. It is not, however, that Iago does not believe in virtue or in love, rather that he wishes to destroy them because he does not possess them, and herein lies another contrast, between his self-concern and Desdemona's selflessness. So too the implicit pruriency of his references to sex stands in direct contrast to Desdemona's purity, as his deviousness contrasts with her honesty.

Although Desdemona and Iago function as representatives of goodness and evil, care should be taken when looking at them in this way not to neglect consideration of the ways in which Shakespeare at the same time gives them individual human qualities so that they are not two-dimensional cardboard figures standing for good and evil, but two credible characters. The fact that her purity stands in direct contrast to Iago's prurient sexual imagination, does not mean that Desdemona lacks sexual feelings or that the sexual dimension is lacking in her relationship with Othello; indeed, his jealousy is surely dependent upon its existence and on Desdemona as a passionate woman. When she asks the Senate to allow her to accompany Othello to Cyprus, she does so because if she remains in Venice the marriage will not be consummated until his return ('The rites for why I love him are bereft me', I. iii. 254). Her first appearance in the play shows her as a mature, assured and brave young woman, prepared to face her father, to speak in public, to express her feelings for Othello, and to make a case for accompanying him to the war. We have insights into her activity as manager of her father's household in the same scene, and all this suggests her endurance of suffering later in the play does not result from weakness and passivity, or an inability to protest. Though she is admittedly a relatively more simply-drawn character than Othello or Iago, nevertheless her human complexity is suggested by the rather ambiguous circumstances of her elopement and marriage which involve the deception of Brabantio by the two characters in the play who are presented as possessing openness and honesty of character. Her lie under pressure to Othello when she tells him that the handkerchief is not lost is also a very human touch, and one which contributes to Othello's suspicion of her. It is Shakespeare's ability to present an ideal in a credible human character which makes the play so tragic. By doing so the dramatist suggests human possibilities for achieving ideals of love and harmony and shows them undermined by equally credible human impulses of envy, mockery and negation in the character of Iago.

4.2.2 Language and imagery

Language and imagery are exceptionally important in the defining of character and in the delineation of the tragic process in *Othello*. Iago and Othello speak in distinctly different ways. The latter speaks predominantly in verse, whilst Iago speaks on many occasions in prose. It is not, however, a matter of a simple verse–prose contrast, and we need to look more closely at the differences. Iago speaks in prose notably when he is talking to Roderigo, or to Cassio in II. iii, but in soliloquy he speaks in blank verse, and at one point in II. i, as he talks to Desdemona about women, he speaks in rhyming couplets. In fact, II. i shows Iago speaking in blank verse, rhyming verse and prose within one scene. It is appropriate to a character who assumes false appearances according to the occasion and the person to whom he is talking. His rhymed couplets indicate his intention to amuse, albeit in a rather mocking and cynical manner; the chiming rhymes present a humorous effect and have a flippant and banal quality (II. i. 147–59). When he next speaks, a few lines later, it is in an aside, his thoughts hidden from others, threatening and sinister in implication as he watches Cassio take Desdemona's hand. The utterance changes to prose as he provides a commentary on what he observes. The contrast with the preceding rhyming verse is very distinct and emphatic, underlining the evil and hatred which lie behind the apparently pleasant and rather mindlessly humorous exterior. When he next speaks it is to Roderigo and again in prose, and this section of dialogue follows the elevated blank verse of Othello's arrival and greeting to Desdemona, again providing an emphatic contrast. At the end of the scene Iago, in soliloquy, speaks in blank verse, but the quality is very different from the blank verse Shakespeare gives to Othello. Iago's has a certain 'prosaic' quality. It is closer to ordinary speech, both in its lack of developed imagery and in its rhythms. The phrases are often short and direct, and the speech moves with a reasoned logic. Notice the opening of the soliloquy:

> That Cassio loves her, I do well believe't;
> That she loves him, 'tis apt and of great credit.
> The Moor – howbeit that I endure him not –
> Is of a constant, loving, noble nature,
> And I dare think he'll prove to Desdemona
> A most dear husband. (290–5)

The punctuation indicates how broken the lines are and how short-breathed are the phrases. It is direct and unembellished with imagery, as if he is saying, 'These are the facts'. If you set this against Othello's greeting of Desdemona in the same scene you will find a considerable difference –

> O my soul's joy!
> If after every tempest come such calms,
> May the winds blow till they have wakened death,
> And let the labouring bark climb hills of seas
> Olympus-high, and duck again as low
> As hell's from heaven. If it were now to die,
> 'Twere now to be most happy; for I fear
> My soul hath her content so absolute
> That not another comfort like to this
> Succeeds in unknown fate. (182–91)

This is passionate, not reasoned, utterance. The exclamation, 'O my soul's joy!', indicates the passion behind the words. The length of the two sentences which follow, both of almost five lines each, with the flow of the second unbroken from the semi-colon onwards, contrasts with the shorter phrasing of Iago's speech, and their onward flow conveys the impression of passionate feelings. Moreover, Othello's speech reveals a vivid pictorial imagination, for which things have symbolic significance. The literal storm and the calm which have followed it become images which express the torment of being separated from his beloved and his joy at being reunited with her. The extremes of heights and depths, expressed through the image of the ship climbing 'hills of seas' convey the intensity of the contrasting emotions which he has experienced on the journey to, and on the arrival at, Cyprus. For Iago, with his cynical materialistic vision, the world consists of things, and things which are quite separate from himself. In his soliloquy it is significant that when he does use a striking image it is a simile – 'the thought whereof/Doth, like a poisonous mineral, gnaw my inwards'. A simile keeps the two things being compared quite distinct and separate, whereas metaphor brings them together by speaking of one thing in terms of the other. Othello's ability to use metaphor and symbol suggests, by contrast to Iago, a mind capable of investing phenomena with emotional or spiritual significance, and of finding connections between himself and the world in which he lives, making it part of his internal world. Metaphor expresses Othello's oneness with his world.

As Othello's sea references in the speech quoted above indicate, his characteristic imagery tends to refer to the wider world and to the elements of nature, travel and military exploits, reflecting his earlier life, whereas Iago's more limited use of imagery refers to a more limited everyday world. There is one moment when Iago speaks with a hint of the language of Othello, and it is, significantly, at a moment when he wishes to convince the Moor that he is at one with him. At the end of III. iii, when Iago suggests that his master may change his mind about taking vengeance on Cassio, Othello swears otherwise in a speech which exhibits his characteristically sweeping phrases, elemental imagery and wide views, 'Like to the Pontic sea . . . '. As he says

> Now, by yond marble heaven,
> In the due reverence of a sacred vow
> I here engage my words

he kneels, and Iago also kneels, echoing his words –

> Witness, you ever-burning lights above,
> You elements that clip us round about,
> Witness that here Iago doth give up
> The execution of his wit, hands, heart,
> To wronged Othello's service. (III. iii. 458–62).

This is yet another verbal instance of Iago's adaptability, of his talent for creating false impressions. He speaks in Othello's language to try to convince his master that he is at one with him.

As Othello becomes affected by Iago's mental poison, his utterances become in various ways more like those of the ensign. It may not be accident that though the 'Like to the Pontic sea' speech is characteristic of Othello in many respects, it is based upon a simile rather than a metaphor which separates rather than brings together the things being compared. More clearly, earlier in the scene, in the central soliloquy, we find the poisoning of Othello's mind expressed through the uncharacteristic image of the toad in the dungeon. The

darkness and confinement of the dungeon are in direct contrast to the
open views of the daylight world of sky and sea and distant lands
which we associate with Othello through his earlier speeches, whilst
the association of poison, evil and ugliness which the toad carries
make it a creature we more readily associate with Iago and his evil
designs. It is an image which is repeated by Othello with heightened
feelings of sexual disgust:

> But there where I have garnered up my heart,
> Where either I must live or bear no life,
> The fountain from the which my current runs
> Or else dries up – to be discarded thence,
> Or keep it as a cistern for foul toads
> To knot and gender in! (IV. ii, 56–61).

The recurrence and the development in intensity of this image is
indicative of how Iago's poison is working and how Othello is
becoming more like Iago.

This is also indicated by the fact that in IV. i, after the great
temptation scene of III. iii, and as Iago becomes more daring and
explicit in his statements to Othello, the general's utterance moves
from blank verse into prose, as he observes Cassio talking with Iago
and then with Bianca. The most noticeable use of prose comes just
before he collapses, when he speaks in disjointed prose expressive of
the disintegration of his mental world.

In the final scene of the play, the speeches of Othello express
through reminders of the characteristic utterance of the earlier
Othello, though now impaired and crippled, the tragic process that
has occurred. The opening speech expresses the conflict between a
false rationality which tells him he must kill Desdemona for her
infidelity ('It is the cause, it is the cause, my soul') and a passionate
emotional response which would persuade him to let her live,
intuitively perceiving her 'whiteness' ('that whiter skin of her than
snow,/And smooth as monumental alabaster'). Apparent rationality
has been characteristic of Iago, whereas intuitive understanding of
truths through emotional engagement with people and the world is
characteristic of the noble Othello. The attempt in the 'Behold I have
a weapon' speech to recapture the old days of heroic action,
expressed through the use of sweeping phrasing –

> I have seen the day
> That with this little arm, and this good sword,
> I have made my way through more impediments
> Than twenty times your stop –

breaks down into short phrases as he realises its pointlessness, 'But,

oh vain boast! Who can control his fate?'. Even the sea imagery
which he uses here is brief and direct, 'Here is my journey's end, here
is my butt/And very sea-mark of my utmost sail.' The recurrent
questions, short phrases, and broken lines express his uncertainty,
and the reminders of the earlier Othello which details like the sea
imagery convey, emphasise for us what has been lost. Othello's final
speech restores something of the former eloquence and nobility,
whilst still retaining a sense of that loss. It begins, slowly and quietly,
with short phrases, and in a direct manner – 'Soft you; a word or two
before you go . . . Speak of me as I am' – but as it develops the
phrases of the speech begin to expand and throb with passionate
eloquence. The sentence beginning, 'Then must you speak . . .' is
very long and builds by means of repetition of the words 'of one'. As
it builds, imagery is introduced for the first time, and imagery which
stresses the intensity of the feeling – first the throwing away of the
pearl, the destruction of Desdemona, and then the image of the
Arabian trees, expressive of his intense sorrow. In the final lines past
heroic action and present action are brought together, image and act
are one, as Othello, whose former honour had rested particularly on
his courage and valour as a fighter of the infidel, of external evil, now
destroys the internal evil, the infidel in himself.

4.3 SETTING

The settings of Shakespeare's plays often function at a deeper level
than simply providing a locale in which the events of the play take
place. Frequently they contribute significantly to thematic concerns
and development. It is noticeable how often Shakespeare's plays
present characters moving from one location to another contrasting
environment, and sometimes back again. This feature is found in
works from widely different periods of his writing career, and in plays
of different genres; for instance, in the early comedy, *A Midsummer
Night's Dream* (1596), characters leave the city of Athens at the end
of Act I and the central part of the play takes place in a wood outside
the city, until, finally, the characters return to Athens at the end of
the play; in the tragedy, *King Lear* (1605), the action of the play
moves from the court and the human community to the wild and
desolate heath, inhabited only by the outcasts of society; in the late
romance, *The Winter's Tale* (1611), the action moves from the court
world of Sicilia to the rural world of Bohemia, and finally, back to the
court. Often the different settings suggest areas of new psychological
experience which the characters encounter, and which contribute to
their development. In *A Midsummer Night's Dream*, the release from
the city world of order, reason and harsh restrictive law provided by
the 'wood experience', associated with passion, magic, imagination
and fantasy, enables the lovers to understand their real feelings for

each other thus bringing the play to a harmonious conclusion.

In *Othello* the change of location occurs after Act I when the action moves from Venice to Cyprus. What significance lies in this change? Venice in Shakespeare's day was the wealthy centre of a rich trading empire. It provided an appropriate setting for the comedy, *The Merchant of Venice* (1597), a play concerned with contrasts between material wealth and love's riches. Though *Othello* presents a contrast between the spiritual worth of the love of Othello and Desdemona and the cynical materialism of Iago, the Venetian setting is not used significantly for its associations with wealth and mercantile enterprises, but for the fact that it was a Christian state which, because of its trading empire, found itself frequently in conflict with the Muslim Turks who presented a threat to Europe and to Christendom. In the fifteenth century Venice lost most of its eastern possessions in a war with the Turks. Cyprus, which the Venetians had acquired in 1489 was, in August 1571, taken by the Turks, who treated the defenders with great barbarity. However, in October of the same year, the Venetians, in league with Spain, Genoa, Malta and the Papal States, defeated the whole maritime force of the Turks at the battle of Lepanto and completely checked their progress. This was a cause of great relief to Christian states. The Eastern Roman Empire had ended when Constantinople was taken by the Turks under Mahomet II in May 1453. Greece came under Turkish subjection by 1460. The Sultan, Solyman the Magnificent, captured Belgrade in August 1521, and the island of Rhodes in December of the following year. Seven years later he laid siege to Vienna, though he was unsuccessful in taking the city. Vienna was again besieged by the Turks as late as 1683, though again unsuccessfully. It will be evident from all this that the Turks were a constant menace to Christian Europe.

Shakespeare sets his tragedy of *Othello* against the background of this conflict, and the characteristics of the opposing states are linked to the thematic concerns of the play. The Turks are the infidel, the unbelievers, the enemies of the true religion. They are barbarous, cunning and deceptive. Venice, by contrast, is a civilised Christian state. It is significant that the third scene of Act I presents the Venetian Senate, the body which governs the state, and which in the case of Brabantio against Othello becomes a court of law in which the Duke as judge tries to get at the truth of the accusations against the Moor. Venice is associated with government, reason and law in this scene. It is also the place where Othello, whose military exploits have taken him to distant parts of the world, finds love for the first time. It is a place of solid stable structures, not simply in its government, but in its domestic life, as the references to Brabantio's household by Othello indicate. It is the heart of the Venetian empire and is not itself directly threatened by the Turkish forces. Cyprus, on the other hand, is an outpost of empire, on the very verges of civilisation where Christian and Turk confront each other. When Othello and Desdemona leave Venice, they leave a secure and familiar world for the unfamiliar and precarious situation of Cyprus where civilisation ends and barbarism begins, an embattled island rather than a seat of government, which the forces of savagery and evil might easily engulf. We may see the settings of Venice and Cyprus as linked to the personal situation of the lovers. In Venice, Iago's attempts at disruption are prevented by the reason, justice and orderly conduct of the Venetian senate; societal structures and institutions keep at bay the forces of disorder and evil. In Cyprus, however, Othello and Desdemona have only their own resources on which to rely, and they are therefore more vulnerable to irrationality and deception.

The change of location also symbolically reflects the change in the lives of Othello and Desdemona as a result of their love and marriage. Despite the approval which the play seems to give to the marriage, Desdemona's elopement may be viewed as an action which contravenes the rules of society, and which undermines authority in the figure of Brabantio, who should have been asked for his daughter's hand. Though the Venetian Senate gives its approval, and Shakespeare himself does not provide a perspective which presents the actions of the lovers in a clearly critical light, we are nevertheless aware that their love puts strains upon the very societal structures which would be its chief preservers. The Duke condemns the action until he knows that it is Othello who is involved, the very person of whom the state has most need in its political crisis. Justice is compromised by expediency as a result of the lovers' action. Brabantio's parting words, 'Look to her, Moor, if thou hast eyes to see:/She has deceived her father, and may thee', which are echoed later by Iago in III. iii, also have an unsettling effect by drawing attention to the breaking of social rules and to the fact that the open and honest Othello has been involved in an action of deception. Shakespeare does not linger over this, as the scene seems to be drawing to a harmonious conclusion with the Duke's attempts to make things right, but we have a sense that all is not quite well, and that the lovers are less secure than they might seem at this point.

The change of setting also reflects their personal situation in another way. To love someone deeply is to expose oneself to the possibility of being deeply hurt. The person who is emotionally unattached, as Othello has been until this time, is not vulnerable in the same way. Their relationship involves them entering new and unfamiliar areas of experience, emotionally and physically. Not only does Othello change his single state for marriage and link himself with the personal and domestic world, but Desdemona, who has lived her life until this moment in the familiar environment of her father's Venetian household, suddenly is alienated from her father and is transported to a distant place, as well as having, like Othello, the new experience of marriage.

By making the central character of the tragedy a Moor rather than a Venetian, and by subverting audience stereotyped expectations about the behaviour of the black man, Shakespeare presents Othello as a man who has his origins in a pagan society (his speech about the magic of the handkerchief indicates this) and who has been in contact with savage peoples (the cannibals), but who has come under the civilising influence of a Christian society. The audience can believe that the tumultuous passions and latent violence, which through the familiar stereotype are understood to be associated with the black man, are kept in check by the restraints of civilisation, and, indeed, the Othello of the first act is distinguished by his control and calm assurance, appearing, in contrast to Iago and Brabantio, a perfect example of civilised man. Away from Venice and all that it represents, Iago can more easily work to undo the influence of civilisation and to release the latent forces of savagery and violence, which the contemporary audience believed the black man to possess. The setting in Cyprus, at the edges of the civilised world, so vulnerable to the forces of barbarism, is appropriate to the psychological situation.

5 SPECIMEN CRITICAL ANALYSIS

OTHELLO Most potent, grave and reverend signiors,
  My very noble and approved good masters:
  That I have ta'en away this old man's daughter,
  It is most true; true I have married her;
  The very head and front of my offending
  Hath this extent, no more. Rude am I in my speech,
  And little blessed with the soft phrase of peace;
  For since these arms of mine had seven years' pith,
  Till now, some nine moons wasted, they have used
  Their dearest action in the tented field;
  And little of this great world can I speak
  More than pertains to feats of broils and battle;
  And therefore little shall I grace my cause
  In speaking for myself. Yet by your gracious patience,
  I will a round unvarnished tale deliver
  Of my whole course of love: what drugs, what charms,
  What conjuration, and what mighty magic –
  For such proceeding I am charged withal –
  I won his daughter.   (I. iii. 76–94)

Othello's address to the Venetian Senate to defend himself against Brabantio's accusations of having bewitched Desdemona provides another indication of his calmness, assurance and openness, which were demonstrated in his first appearance in the preceding scene. It stands in contrast to the more emotional and agitated utterances of Brabantio as he seeks the Senate's aid. Though Othello says that he is not accomplished as a public speaker ('Rude am I in my speech'), the speech strikes one as that of a person who does have oratorical skills and who knows how to be persuasive with words. It is chiefly sentence structure and rhythms which create this impression. The first two lines are taken up with showing respect for the senators. The number of complimentary words – potent, grave, reverend, noble, good – indicates a desire to draw a favourable response from them, and might even suggest a degree of flattery. The indication, too, of their superiority – they are the masters, he the servant – further enforces this. Although Brabantio is also a senator, Othello's words set him apart and establish a contrast between the 'potent' signiors and 'this old man', impotently complaining at his daughter's marriage to the Moor. We might see a hint of disrespect here, though we should have to bear in mind Othello's respectful treatment of Brabantio in the previous scene. There does, however, seem to be something of an attempt on Othello's part to get the senators on to his side and to set Brabantio apart as the outsider in the situation. The weight and dignity of the first two lines about the senators, achieved through the building of one complimentary adjective upon another, stands in stark contrast to the bluntness of the phrase, 'this old man's daughter', in the third line. You might consider in what ways the effect would have been different if instead he had said, 'Desdemona' or 'Brabantio's daughter'.

Othello goes on emphasise that he is not going to hide anything; he admits the truth of the accusation that he has taken away and married Desdemona, repeating the word, 'true'. Shakespeare constructs the line so that the two 'trues' are placed together for emphatic purposes, and the placing of 'no more' at the end of a sentence and in the middle of a verse line, necessitating a pause, gives it emphasis, and enforces the assertion that Brabantio's claims of witchcraft are unfounded. So quite concisely and emphatically Othello admits to the Senate what he has done and denies the accusation of having used magic.

The next lines serve to emphasise Othello as the soldier and man of action, and implicitly to remind the Senate of its need for him at a time when it is facing the Turkish threat. Contrasts are established: 'Speech' and 'the soft phrase of peace' are set against 'action in the tented field'. The senators whose concern with government means that verbal debate is a familiar activity for them must make allowances for the inexperience in these matters of one whose past experience, since he was a child, has made him accomplished in the sphere of military action rather than of words. The phrases 'the soft phrase of peace', and 'dearest action' also suggest another contrast. His arms have been used in fighting since an early age; 'dearest action', that is, what he has enjoyed doing most, has been fighting. The reference to 'arms' and 'dearest action' in this context, however, make us think of the arms as those of the lover as well as of the warrior. The emphatic placing of 'Till now' at the beginning of line 84 points to the change that has occurred in Othello. Something important has happened to change his life. The implication of the lines is that until this time he had not been a lover, and that through this contrast of what he was and what he is, Othello seeks to emphasise to the Senate that his elopement with and marriage to Desdemona have not been frivolous actions, but are the result of a love so serious and important that it could change the pattern of his life. A further contrast is perhaps implicit in the phrase 'the tented field'; the tents (impermanent dwellings) of the military camp suggesting a contrast to the stability and permanence of a domestic household such as Othello by marrying would need to establish in Venice. The following speech of Othello, in which he describes his visits to Brabantio's house, presents such a household. Though Othello says he knows little of 'this great world', suggesting limitations of experience in human affairs, he clearly establishes himself in this speech as connected with a wider world into which he goes, or is sent, on military missions, in contrast to the world of the Venetian senators. This is a contrast which is fully established in his next speech. So, very subtly, these lines, whilst on one level stating Othello's limitations and lack of experience, enforce a sense of the exceptional nature of Othello and of his love for Desdemona, and perhaps force upon the senators a sense of their own limitations, that Othello, in some respects, knows more of 'this great world' than they who remain at home in Venice.

Having stated that he lacks oratorical skills to present his case effectively, Othello then proceeds to state that, if they are prepared to listen to him none the less ('by your gracious patience'), he will tell them plainly how he won Desdemona's love. The use of the phrase, 'round, unvarnished tale' sets up other contrasts. First, it suggests an implicit contrast to the tale he would have told if he had had the oratorical skills which he protests he lacks; thus he subtly implies a connection between eloquence and power to deceive. Because he lacks eloquence, he implies, the senators are actually more likely to hear the truth. The tale will be 'unvarnished', suggesting that it will lack any embellishment, and will not be made to seem other than it is. Thus he suggests plainness and directness in contrast to the deviousness of which Brabantio has accused him in his accusations of witchcraft. The contrast is between openness and underhand dealings. By repetition of 'what' and the building of one thing upon another – 'What drugs, what charms,/What conjuration, and what mighty magic' – Othello reminds the Senate that he has been accused of dark and mysterious practices, whilst the whole speech enforces a sense of his plainness, openness and honesty, that the plain statement with which the speech ends, 'I won his daughter', standing in contrast to the oratorical nature of the list of accusations preceding it, emphatically underlines.

As this analysis shows, this speech has complex implications and undertones. It raises the possibility of a range of interpretations in performance. To what extent should we take Othello at his word that he lacks the verbal skills of persuasion for putting his case, when this speech, and the next in which he describes how he won Desdemona's love, are so successfully persuasive? To what extent do his protestations of directness, openness and of telling a 'round, unvarnished tale' actually hide subtle implications intended to manipulate the Senate? Do the opening lines show deep respect for the senators or are they calculated flattery? Repeatedly Shakespeare's text raises such questions of interpretation. Othello's final speech containing his description of himself as 'not easily jealous' has provided a focus for much discussion, but elsewhere in the play speeches such as that considered here raise similar problems. There is a certain mystery about the character of Othello as there is about the character of Iago, and consequently the possible range of interpretation offered by the text to the director or actor is considerable. Martin L. Wine in the *Othello* volume of the Macmillan Text and Performance series (see '*Further Reading*') writes thus of Sir Laurence Olivier's interpretation of this speech in 1964, 'His address to the Senators is polite enough, but a shade too flattering to be thought totally sincere. His words say one thing, but, as Olivier utters them, they seem to point to a scarcely disguised contempt for an effete white society and its 'curled darlings'. The Senators, who need his military capability, are not at ease. This Othello knows that he is playing a role, that he is dramatising himself: he is in complete control' (Wine, pp. 49–50). The writer indicates by the words 'as Olivier utters them', that the same lines, spoken in a different way by another actor, could present us with a different view of the character, one for instance who was totally sincere.

6 CRITICAL RECEPTION AND INTERPRETATION

The range of interpretation which Shakespeare's text allows is evident in the division of critical opinion. The problem of Othello and how we should view him – as hero or fool, noble or self-regarding – encourages different responses from critics and from actors and directors. Martin Wine says 'of Shakespeare's four tragic heroes, Othello remains the least accessible to explanation and understanding' (Wine, p. 11, see 'Further Reading'). Dr Johnson, in the eighteenth century wrote of 'The fiery openness of Othello, magnanimous, artless, and credulous, boundless in his confidence, ardent in his affection, inflexible in his resolution, and obdurate in his revenge'. The traditional view of the noble Moor is to be found most influentially in the twentieth-century critic, A. C. Bradley, in his book, *Shakespearean Tragedy*. Bradley examines character, surveys interpretational options, and then puts his own view which depends upon taking Othello at his own estimate; he writes,

> Othello's nature is all of one piece. His trust, where he trusts, is absolute. Hesitation is almost impossible to him. He is extremely self-reliant, and decides and acts instantaneously. If stirred to indignation . . . he answers with one lightning stroke. Love, if he loves, must be to him the heaven where either he must live or bear no life . . . This character is so noble, Othello's feelings and actions follow so inevitably from it and from the forces brought to bear on it, and his sufferings are so heartrending, that he stirs, I believe, in most readers a passion of mingled love and pity which they feel for no other hero in Shakespeare. (Macmillan Casebook, pp. 60–1)

On the other side, T. S. Eliot presents a view of Othello as a self-dramatiser who is concerned in his final speech with 'cheering himself up'. Eliot writes,

He is endeavouring to escape reality, he has ceased to think about Desdemona, and is thinking of himself. Humility is the most difficult of all virtues to achieve; nothing dies harder than the desire to think well of oneself. Othello succeeds in turning himself into a pathetic figure, by adopting an *aesthetic* rather than a moral attitude, dramatizing himself against his environment. He takes in the spectator, but the human motive is primarily to take in himself. (Macmillan Casebook, p. 70)

Taking up Eliot's suggestion here, F. R. Leavis develops it and makes a criticism of Bradley's approach and view of tragedy, detecting important deficiencies in Othello's character which are evident from the early stages of the play. Replying to Bradley's statement quoted above, Leavis writes,

With such resolute fidelity does Bradley wear these blinkers that he can say,

His trust, where he trusts, is absolute,

without realising the force of the corollary: Othello's trust, then, can never have been in Desdemona. It is the vindication of Othello's perfect nobility that Bradley is preoccupied with, and we are to see the immediate surrender to Iago as part of that nobility. But to make absolute trust in Iago – trust at Desdemona's expense – a manifestation of perfect nobility is . . . to make Iago a very remarkable person indeed. And that, Bradley, tradition aiding and abetting, proceeds to do. (Macmillan Casebook, p. 128)

Leavis wrote that in 1952. Three years later, in a lecture entitled 'The Noble Moor', Dame Helen Gardner countered such a view, saying,

Othello is like a hero of the ancient world in that he is not a man like us, but a man recognized as extraordinary. He seems born to do great deeds and live in legend. He has the obvious heroic qualities of courage and strength . . . He has the heroic capacity for passion . . . His value is not in what the world thinks of him, although the world rates him highly, and does not derive in any way from his station. It is inherent. (Macmillan Casebook, p. 151)

Later in the lecture Helen Gardner rejects the search for a psychological explanation of Othello's downfall,

Iago ruins Othello by insinuating into his mind the question 'How do you know?' The tragic experience with which the play is concerned is loss of faith, and Iago is the instrument to bring Othello to the crisis of his being. . . The strange and extraordinary, the heroic, what is beyond nature, can be made to seem the unnatural, what is against nature. This is one of Iago's tricks. But the collapse of Othello's faith before Iago's hints, refusals, retreats, reluctant avowals, though plausible and circumstantiated, is not, I believe, ultimately explicable; nor do I believe we make it so by searching for some psychological weakness in the hero. . . (Macmillan Casebook, p. 157).

The differing views of Othello inevitably lead to differing views of Iago. If Othello is noble as Bradley sees him, Iago must be a powerful corrupting influence, but if Othello is as Leavis sees him, then Iago is not a character of 'fiendish intellectual superiority' but 'no more than a necessary piece of dramatic mechanism'. Juliet McLauchlan draws together views of Iago which see him as connected with the Vice figure from mediaeval morality plays, with the Devil, with the Machiavel or cunning manipulator and plotter, and with the type of the bluff soldier. There is, however, less controversy over the essential nature of Iago than over Othello. Most critics agree that he expresses a spirit of negation.

The fault of the Bradley and of the Leavis views is that they see Othello in extreme terms as either noble or as self-deceiving fool. In his essay, 'The Modern Othello' (*English Literary History*, 2 (1944), reprinted in L. F. Dean (ed.), *A Casebook on 'Othello'*, New York, 1961), Leo Kirschbaum acknowledges the need to appreciate the complexity of the character, and suggests 'It is the close interweaving of great man, mere man, and base man that makes of Othello the powerful and mysterious figure he is.' However, few critics manage to bring the two polarised views of Othello together to explore this complexity, but in a recent study of the play, *Othello as Tragedy: Some problems of judgment and feeling*, Jane Adamson argues against the simplicity which the polarisation encourages. She presents Othello as a complex tragic figure, and considers moral questions which are raised by the play. Because the interpretation of the character of Othello is so difficult, critics who have attempted to consider the play from the point of view of its moral significance have had problems. One of the earliest attempts was made by Thomas Rymer at the end of the seventeenth century in his *Short View of Tragedy* (1692). Frustrated in his attempts to find any moral significance in *Othello*, he mockingly declared that it presented 'a warning to all good wives, that they look well to their Linen' and 'a lesson to Husbands, that before their Jealousie be Tragical, the proofs may be mathematical.' For Harley Granville-Barker in this century, the play seemed 'a tragedy without meaning, and that is the ultimate horror of it'.

Attention to the language of the play is given by G. Wilson Knight in the chapter 'The Othello Music', in *The Wheel of Fire*; by William Empson in a chapter, ' "Honest" in *Othello*', in *The Structure of Complex Words*; and R. B. Heilman in *Magic in the Web: Action and Language in 'Othello'*. Wilson Knight shows how the Miltonic music of Othello is untuned and made discordant by Iago's cynicism and rationality. The Othello music conveys a sense of the heroic and the magnificent. However, Leavis with his anti-heroic view, suggests that it is Othello's own way of investing himself with romantic glamour, of dramatising himself.

In the theatre, interpretation has been as divided as academic criticism. Examination of theatrical interpretations is made in Marvin Rosenberg's *The Masks of Othello*. There is a tendency in this book to suggest that there is a basic identity for each character which has to be found by the actor, so that their complexity and the range of possible interpretations are not fully suggested. Of twentieth-century productions, the two which assume the greatest importance, and which attract most frequent comment, presented diametrically opposed views of the central character. The first was Margaret Webster's production with the black singer and actor Paul Robeson in the title role, in the 1943–4 Broadway season. Robeson had earlier appeared in another production in London, but the significance of the Broadway production lay in the fact that for the first time in America a black actor was playing with an all-white cast. Robeson wrote about these performances in 'Some Reflections on *Othello* and the Nature of our Time' (*American Scholar*, 14 (1945)) and commented that American audiences found the play

strikingly contemporary in its overtones of a clash of cultures, of the partial acceptance of and consequent effect upon one of a minority group. Against this background the jealousy of the protagonist becomes more credible, the blows to his pride more understandable, the final collapse of his personal, individual world, more inevitable.

Robeson gave a 'romantic' interpretation of the noble Moor. By contrast, Sir Laurence Olivier's 'realistic' interpretation in John Dexter's production at the National Theatre in 1964 presented the Othello of Leavis's essay, a self-dramatising egotist. This production was made into a film. Such transference from the evanescent medium of the theatre to the more permanent medium of the film has meant that this production has been seen by many more people and has been influential either in confirming for some people a particular critical viewpoint or provoking in others a reaction against it.

REVISION QUESTIONS

The purpose of these questions is to help you to develop your understanding of the play more fully by exploring important aspects in depth. They may provide a focus for your own private study, or a basis for discussion with others, or you might use them for written answers. Writing an answer will make you sort out and develop your ideas and will sometimes make you realise that points you thought you had understood have not been fully grasped.

1. Tragic victim or agent of his fate? To what extent do you consider Othello is to blame for his own downfall?

2. Dr Johnson suggested that the play would have been better if the first act, set in Venice, had been omitted. Do you agree with him?

3. Would you accept the view that we cannot believe in any of the three main characters – Iago is too evil, Desdemona is too good, and Othello is too gullible?

4. By what means does Shakespeare convey the main characteristics of the love of Othello and Desdemona?

5. Consider the dramatic importance of one of the following characters: Brabantio, Roderigo or Cassio.

6. How adequate is it to describe *Othello* as simply a domestic tragedy?

7. To what extent is Iago's success dependent upon other factors than his own cleverness?

8. '*Othello* is about relationship and isolation: we are presented with a bleak world of isolated and alienated individuals, and of broken relationships, lighted only for a brilliant but brief moment by the mutual love of Othello and Desdemona.' Examine and discuss this view of the play.

9. In what different ways is imagery important in *Othello*? You may consider visual as well as verbal imagery if you wish.

10. To what extent do you accept Othello's description of himself as 'one not easily jealous, but being wrought,/Perplexed in the extreme'?

11. Examine irony as an important effect in the tragedy.

12. How important are time and place in *Othello*?

13. Examine some of the effects that Shakespeare creates through scenic juxtaposition in *Othello*.

14. Take a scene from the play and write an account of it from the point of view of one of the characters involved, indicating his or her thoughts when in the text Shakespeare provides no words for the character. When you have done this write an account of the scene from the point of view of another character who is present, considering carefully in what ways the events affect the two characters differently and evoke different responses.

APPENDIX:

SHAKESPEARE'S THEATRE

BY HAROLD BROOKS

We should speak, as Muriel Bradbrook reminds us, not of the Elizabethan stage but of Elizabethan stages. Plays of Shakespeare were acted on tour, in the halls of mansions, one at least in Gray's Inn, frequently at Court, and after 1609 at the Blackfriars, a small roofed theatre for those who could afford the price. But even after his Company acquired the Blackfriars, we know of no play of his not acted (unless, rather improbably, *Troilus* is an exception) for the general public at the Globe, or before 1599 at its predecessor, The Theatre, which, since the Globe was constructed from the same timbers, must have resembled it. Describing the Globe, we can claim therefore to be describing, in an acceptable sense, Shakespeare's theatre, the physical structure his plays were designed to fit. Even in the few probably written for a first performance elsewhere, adaptability to that structure would be in his mind.

For the facilities of the Globe we have evidence from the drawing of the Swan theatre (based on a sketch made by a visitor to London about 1596) which depicts the interior of another public theatre; the builder's contract for the Fortune theatre, which in certain respects (fortunately including the dimensions and position of the stage) was to copy the Globe; indications in the dramatic texts; comments, like Ben Jonson's on the throne let down from above by machinery; and eye-witness testimony to the number of spectators (in round figures, 3000) accommodated in the auditorium.

In communicating with the audience, the actor was most favourably placed. Soliloquising at the centre of the front of the great platform, he was at the mid-point of the theatre, with no one among the spectators more than sixty feet away from him. That platform-stage (Figs I and II) was the most important feature for performance at the Globe. It had the audience – standing in the yard (10) and seated in the galleries (9) – on three sides of it. It was 43 feet wide, and $27\frac{1}{2}$ feet from front to back. Raised ($5\frac{1}{2}$ feet) above the level of the yard, it had a trap-door (II.8) giving access to the space below it. The

SHAKESPEARE'S THEATRE

The stage and its adjuncts; the tiring-house; and the auditorium.

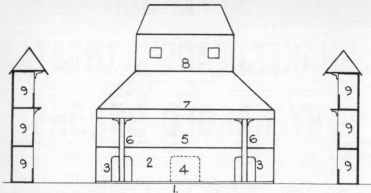

FIG I ELEVATION
1. Platform stage (approximately five feet above the ground) 2. Tiring-house
3. Tiring-house doors to stage 4. Conjectured third door 5. Tiring-house
gallery (balustrade and partitioning not shown) 6. Pillars supporting the
heavens 7. The heavens 8. The hut 9. The spectators' galleries

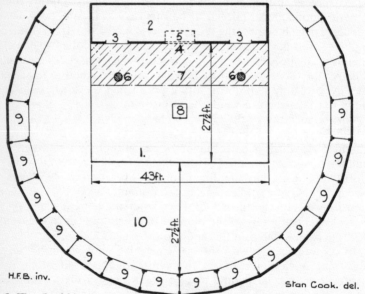

H.F.B. inv.   Stan Cook. del.

FIG II PLAN
1. Platform stage 2. Tiring-house 3. Tiring-house doors to stage
4. Conjectural third door 5. Conjectural discovery space (alternatively behind 3)
6. Pillars supporting the heavens 7. The heavens 8. Trap door 9. Spectators'
gallery 10. The yard

The Globe

An artist's imaginative recreation of a typical Elizabethan theatre

actors, with their equipment, occupied the 'tiring house' (attiring house: 2) immediately at the back of the stage. The stage-direction 'within' means inside the tiring-house. Along its frontage, probably from the top of the second storey, juts out the canopy or 'Heavens', carried on two large pillars rising through the platform (6, 7) and sheltering the rear part of the stage, the rest of which, like the yard, was open to the sky. If the 'hut' (1.8) housing the machinery for descents, stood, as in the Swan drawing, above the 'Heavens', that covering must have had a trap-door, so that the descents could be made through it.

Descents are one illustration of the vertical dimension the dramatist could use to supplement the playing-area of the great platform. The other opportunities are provided by the tiring-house frontage or facade. About this facade the evidence is not so complete or clear as we should like, so that Fig. 1 is in part conjectural. Two doors giving entry to the platform there certainly were (3). A third (4) is probable but not certain. When curtained, a door, most probably this one, would furnish what must be termed a discovery-space (II.5), not an inner stage (on which action in any depth would have been out of sight for a significant part of the audience). Usually no more than two actors were revealed (exceptionally, three), who often then moved out on to the platform. An example of this is Ferdinand and Miranda in *The Tempest* 'discovered' at chess, then seen on the platform speaking with their fathers. Similarly the gallery (1.5) was not an upper stage. Its use was not limited to the actors: sometimes it functioned as 'lords' rooms' for favoured spectators, sometimes, perhaps, as a musicians' gallery. Frequently the whole gallery would not be needed for what took place aloft: a window-stage (as in the first balcony scene in *Romeo*, even perhaps in the second) would suffice. Most probably this would be a part (at one end) in the gallery itself; or just possibly, if the gallery did not (as it does in the Swan drawing) extend the whole width of the tiring-house, a window in the left or right-hand door. As the texts show, whatever was presented aloft, or in the discovery-space, was directly related to the action on the platform, so that at no time was there left, between the audience and the action of the drama, a great bare space of platform-stage. In relating Shakespeare's drama to the physical conditions of the theatre, the primacy of that platform is never to be forgotton.

Note: The present brief account owes most to C. Walter Hodges, *The Globe Restored*; Richard Hosley in *A New Companion to Shakespeare Studies*, and in *The Revels History of English Drama*; and to articles by Hosley and Richard Southern in *Shakespeare Survey*, 12, 1959, where full discussion can be found.

HAROLD BROOKS

FURTHER READING

The following editions of the play have interesting introductions:
Arden edition, ed. M. R. Ridley (Methuen, 1958)
New Cambridge edition, ed. Norman Sanders, (Cambridge University Press, 1984)
New Penguin edition, ed. Kenneth Muir (Penguin, 1968)
Signet edition, ed. Alvin Kernan (New American Library, 1963)

Selected critical works

Adamson, Jane, *Othello as Tragedy: Some problems of judgment and feeling* (Cambridge University Press, 1980). A full-length study of the play which attempts to escape from the polarisation of much past criticism.

Clemen, Wolfgang, *The Development of Shakespeare's Imagery* (Methuen, 1951, reprinted 1977), ch. 13.

Heilman, R. B., *Magic in the Web: Action and Language in 'Othello'* (Kentucky University Press, 1956). Provides a full examination of language and imagery.

Holloway, John, *The Story of the Night* (Routledge, 1961). The chapter on *Othello* provides a favourable view of the central character and a close examination of the central scene (III. iii.) which strengthens the case against accusations that Othello is easily jealous.

Jones, Eldred, *Othello's Countrymen: The African in English Renaissance Drama* (Oxford University Press, 1965). Useful if you want to know more about black characters in the drama of the period and about the prejudices of the audience.

McLauchlan, Juliet, *Shakespeare's 'Othello'* (Edward Arnold: Studies in English Literature Series, 1971). Presents a short but detailed study of important issues and moments in the play, and a view of Othello as noble.

Muir, Kenneth, (ed.), *Aspects of 'Othello'* (Cambridge University Press, 1977). A number of varied and useful essays from *Shakespeare Survey*.

Rosenberg, Marvin, *The Masks of Othello: The Search for the Identity of Othello, Iago and Desdemona by Three Centuries of Actors and Critics* (University of California Press, 1961). Provides a theatrical perspective.

Wain, John (ed.), *Shakespeare: 'Othello'* (Macmillan Casebook Series, 1971). Brings together influential essays expressing conflicting views of the play.

Wine, Martin. L., *'Othello': Text and Performance* (Macmillan, 1984). A useful examination of the text in relation to some contrasting interpretations in the theatre.